To:

_____

From:

_____

Date:

_____

A YEAR OF OF
GRACE

ANGUS BUCHAN

CHRISTIAN ART
PUBLISHERS

Published by Christian Art Publishers
PO Box 1599, Vereeniging, 1930, RSA

© 2019
First edition 2019

Cover designed by Christian Art Publishers

Images used under license from Shutterstock.com

Unless otherwise indicated, all Scripture quotations are taken from the New King James Version®. Copyright © 1979, 1980, 1982 by Thomas Nelson, Inc.
Used by permission. All rights reserved.
Scripture quotations marked KJV are taken from the *Holy Bible*, King James Version, and are in the public domain.
Scripture quotations marked NLT are taken from the *Holy Bible*,
New Living Translation, copyright © 1996, 2004, 2015 by Tyndale House Foundation.
Used by permission of Tyndale House Publishers, Inc., Carol Stream, Illinois 60188.
All rights reserved.
Scripture quotations marked The Message are taken from The Message,
copyright © 1993, 1994, 1995, 1996, 2000, 2001, 2002 by Eugene H. Peterson.
Used by permission of NavPress. All rights reserved.

Set in 14 on 16 pt Palatino LT Std
by Christian Art Publishers

Printed in China

ISBN 978-1-4321-2842-5

19 20 21 22 23 24 25 26 27 28 – 10 9 8 7 6 5 4 3 2 1

From His *abundance*

we have all received

one *gracious blessing*

after another.

~ John 1:16

January

"*My grace is sufficient for you,
for My strength is made perfect in weakness.*"

~ 2 Corinthians 12:9 ~

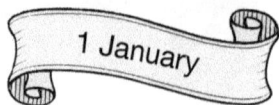

Heeding God's Call

"For everyone to whom much is given, from him much will be required; and to whom much has been committed, of him they will ask the more."

~ Luke 12:48

It is the most wonderful thing to meet the Lord Jesus Christ as your personal Saviour. He says to us very clearly in John 15:16, "You did not choose Me, but I chose you and appointed you that you should go and bear fruit, and that your fruit should remain, that whatever you ask the Father in My name He may give you." This means that God chose us and appointed us to do a specific task.

When God gives us a responsibility and a mandate, we need to fulfil it. We cannot say we love Jesus and then live as we please. We have to be good examples to our fellow man and look after that which God has put in our care. People are watching us all the time; in the way we live, how we lead our families and conduct our businesses.

We have been given much by God – much favour and blessings – and He has washed us clean from all our sins, but with that comes accountability. We need to be good stewards of what God has put in our lives.

An Attitude of Gratitude

I will worship toward Your holy temple, and praise Your name for Your lovingkindness and Your truth; for You have magnified Your word above all Your name. In the day when I cried out, You answered me, and made me bold with strength in my soul.

~ Psalm 138:2-3

We are sometimes very slow to thank God for His continued blessing upon us. Don't grumble because you don't get what you want; be grateful that you don't get what you deserve.

We need to start thanking God for the small blessings and the big ones: to be able to observe Creation every day of our lives. To be able to go for a horse ride, or a bike ride or a jog with your children. To reap the fruits of our labours. We have so many things to be thankful for, yet very few express that gratitude to our Heavenly Father.

Let us, in the coming year, be people who are grateful for the blessings of God. It is a great idea to sit down with a cup of coffee and count your blessings, and to name them one by one. You will be surprised how good God has been to you.

May God bless you, as you cultivate a grateful heart.

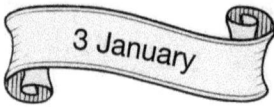

Getting Our Priorities Straight

"For what will it profit a man if he gains the whole world, and loses his own soul?"

~ Mark 8:36

I heard a sad story of a very wealthy man who was ill and slipped into a coma. When he woke up from his coma the first thing he asked for was his laptop, not his family. He wanted to see how the markets were doing. How tragic. The man died a few weeks later.

Maybe you too are overly concerned about your bank balance, about your investments, about your possessions, about your achievements in life. Remember then the words of Mark 8:36, "What will it profit a man if he gains the whole world, and loses his own soul?" The Lord Jesus Christ is more important that anything or anyone in this world.

We need to get our priorities straight and put God first, our family second and then the rest of the world. I encourage you, while God is still giving us time on earth, to get your priorities in order.

You cannot take anything with you when you leave this earth. Therefore, let us not strive for things which are temporal, but rather after the things with eternal value.

Let us take heed and let us change our ways.

Ask Anything in His Name

"If you ask anything in My name, I will do it."

~ John 14:14

Of course this statement does not include selfish requests. It means asking things according to God's nature. If you love the Lord, then you will only ask those things which would be beneficial to the Kingdom of God and to your fellow man.

I have no problem with God blessing people with money. In fact, I have some very wealthy friends, but they are men and women who love Jesus Christ very much and their money has not become an idol. God will not tolerate anything that we give priority over Him. He alone is sovereign. Whatever you ask God for, make sure that your motives are pure and that it will serve to build the Kingdom.

We really need to start implementing practical daily prayer times, starting early in the morning. Praying not only for your farm or business, but also for the personal well-being and needs of your staff.

Let us ask according to God's will and bring glory to the name of Jesus Christ. Let our prayers also be prayers that will assist others to proclaim the Gospel of Jesus Christ, because time is running out and we need to work efficiently and effectively.

Don't Worry

"Therefore I say to you, do not worry about your life, what you will eat; nor about the body, what you will put on."

~ Luke 12:22

The Lord says that we are not to worry about our lives; what we will eat, or what clothes we will put on, because life is more important than food and the body more important than clothing.

The Lord continues in Luke 12:24, "Consider the ravens, for they neither sow nor reap, which have neither storehouse nor barn; and God feeds them. Of how much more value are you than the birds?" I believe this is a very relevant question for us today. We know that people today are suffering a lot from mental disease, depression, stress, anxiety and fear and it all stems from worrying about the future.

The Lord goes on to say we shouldn't be concerned about what we are going to eat or drink because these are the things that the world worries about. Our Heavenly Father knows exactly what we need every day, so rather "seek first the kingdom of God and His righteousness, and all these things shall be added to you" (Matt. 6:33).

Let's put our faith in Him and enjoy each day as it comes, because tomorrow is in God's hands and yesterday is gone. Thanks be to God.

Godly Success

Delight yourself also in the LORD, and He shall give you the desires of your heart.

~ Psalm 37:4

Everywhere I look today the world seems to be absolutely committed to doing things successfully. Whether it be in sports, business, education, or in family life. We are all concerned about being successful in the eyes of the world.

People often say to Christians, "You are so lucky that things always go so well for you." The truth is, everything doesn't always go well for us, but when we do it God's way, obeying His Ten Commandments, He will help us. If we look at John 14:14, Jesus says, "If you ask anything in My name, I will do it." That is one tremendous promise to take hold of as a Christian, but if we look at verse 15, He goes on to say, "If you love Me, keep My commandments."

If, however, we ask for things that are contrary to the Word of God, in other words selfish things that will not bring honour to the Lord Jesus or that will separate us from God, we'll not receive it. However, if we ask according to the Word of God, He will help us.

Jesus loves you and me so much that He wants us to succeed. So let us seek His Kingdom above all else.

Is There a Baal in Your Life?

Therefore, my beloved, flee from idolatry.

~ 1 Corinthians 10:14

The word BAAL is from the Hebrew word BA'AL, which means master or owner. People easily become enslaved to certain things in their lives, like their qualifications, sporting accolades and worldly praise and approval. They don't seem to be able to operate in any other sphere, unless they are doing the thing which they feel fulfils them or makes them successful.

Jesus won't force us to do anything we don't want to do. In Revelation 3:20 we read, "Behold, I stand at the door and knock. If anyone hears My voice and opens the door, I will come in to him and dine with him, and he with Me."

Remember the handle on the door is on the inside and that is why the Lord says that He stands at the door and knocks. If you want Jesus to come into your life and be the Lord of your life, you need to open the door and allow Him in. He will not force the door to try and get in. He will wait for you.

Let us not worship any idols in our lives. The Lord Jesus Christ must be the ultimate Master in our lives.

Christ Transforms You

Therefore, if anyone is in Christ, he is a new creation; old things have passed away; behold, all things have become new.

~ 2 Corinthians 5:17

Transformation in the people of God brings revival. And revival only comes through prayer. Prayer is not something we do only in the morning and in the evening. Prayer is, in fact, a way of life. That is why the Lord tells us in 1 Thessalonians 5:17 to "pray without ceasing."

We need to be consistent with our prayer life if we expect God to move on our behalf. While we pray, we need to be sure that we examine ourselves. Second Corinthians 10:4-5 says, "For the weapons of our warfare are not carnal but mighty in God for pulling down strongholds, casting down arguments and every high thing that exalts itself against the knowledge of God, bringing every thought into captivity to the obedience of Christ."

If we are going to be transformed, we need to start to walk in the Spirit, to pray in the Spirit, to pray all day in the quietness of our hearts and in the workplace. Then God will not only change us, He will change an entire nation.

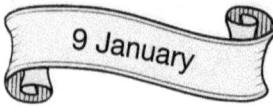

Persistent Faith

Not that I have already attained, or am already perfected; but I press on, that I may lay hold of that for which Christ Jesus has also laid hold of me.

~ Philippians 3:12

As believers, you and I need to be adamant about pursuing God in our lives. Second Kings 2:1-16 tells us how Elisha would not let Elijah go until he received his mantle. Even the sons of the prophets tried to persuade Elisha to leave the man of God, but he refused. He actually told them to keep quiet. He wanted a double portion of the mantle that Elijah had received from God.

The longing to grow closer to the Lord never stops. Paul was a man you would think was satisfied with where he was in his walk with God and yet he still wanted to know the Lord more intimately. He had performed many miracles, signs and wonders, and yet still he longed for a closer walk with God. Paul was persistent in his faith right up until the day that he died.

You and I need to become more persistent followers of Jesus if we want to realise what God has in store for us.

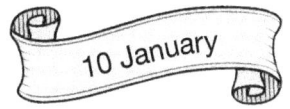

Living Forever in Heaven

I shall not die, but live, and declare the works of the LORD.
~ Psalm 118:17

Paul said in Philippians 1:21, "For to me, to live is Christ, and to die is gain." If we live, we live for Jesus and if we die, we go home to be with Him forever and ever. The apostle Paul knew that he would not die until his mission for Jesus had been completed. I, too, believe that I will not die until my mission on earth has been completed. In fact, not only will I exist, but I will live a fulfilled life. I will stand on God's promises no matter what happens.

Martin Luther once said, "If I knew that tomorrow was the end of the world, I would plant an apple tree today!" Meaning he would continue with his daily chores and life as usual.

They asked John Wesley the same question and he simply responded that he would eat his supper, preach at the candlelight service, say his prayers, and go to bed as usual.

Live as if the Lord is coming back in 1 000 years, but be prepared as if He is coming back today.

No More Fence Sitting

"He who is not with Me is against Me, and he who does not gather with Me scatters abroad."

~ Matthew 12:30

The most uncomfortable place for a believer to be is sitting on the fence. He is neither hot nor cold and Jesus warns us very clearly in Revelation 3:16, "So then, because you are lukewarm, and neither cold nor hot, I will vomit you out of My mouth."

Believers need to be more decisive. There can be no more running with the hares and hunting with the hounds. We are either for Him or against Him.

I think of an account that took place in a Middle Eastern country where Christians were kidnapped by ISIS, a radical terrorist group. The beheading of these 21 believers was recorded for the world to see. These 21 Christians were marched down to the beach and behind each one stood a man dressed in black with a knife. They were killed because they refused to deny Jesus Christ as the Sovereign Lord.

These brave souls chose Jesus over their lives, their families and everything else. They died for Jesus and I am certain He was with them throughout every moment. Let us ask God today, to give us a renewed vision, then we will have a reason to get out of bed in the morning, to roll up our sleeves and to get to work.

Be Anxious for Nothing

Be anxious for nothing, but in everything by prayer and supplication, with thanksgiving, let your requests be made known to God.

~ Philippians 4:6

The opposite of faith is fear. Fear polarises us so that we can't think straight.

We need to start to walk by faith and not by sight (see 2 Cor. 5:7). We must not be concerned about tomorrow because Jesus says that tomorrow has enough concerns of its own. We need to really start to take the Word of God literally.

It's evident how the Lord undertakes for His creation. How true that the lilies of the field are more beautiful than Solomon in all his splendour. Solomon was so well dressed, organised and well-prepared that people came from all over the world to meet him.

Still Jesus said that Solomon in all his splendour did not look as beautiful as the lilies of the field (see Matt. 6:28-30). The Lord reminds us that if He takes care of the birds of the air, how much more will He love us and take care of you and me (see Matt. 10:29-31).

Let us be anxious for nothing as we believe in the Father to provide for us.

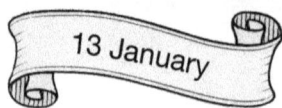

Not Everyone Will Believe

"Father will be divided against son and son against father, mother against daughter and daughter against mother, mother-in-law against her daughter-in-law and daughter-in-law against her mother-in-law."

~ Luke 12:53

We have to face up to the fact that not all of our loved ones will be as committed to Jesus Christ as we would like them to be. It's important to exercise extreme grace, because the Bible tells us in James 5:16, "The effective, fervent prayer of a righteous man avails much."

So if we are patient and prayerful, then by the grace of God they will come back and serve Jesus. In the meantime, this is when we need to spend time on our knees praying on their behalf. We should establish authority in the home and not allow the devil to come in through the back door and cause chaos among our loved ones.

When your children are young you can tell them what to do and what not to do and they must obey, but when they grow up and leave the home, then they have to formulate their own ways and discover what life is all about on their own. If we remain faithful and true to the Lord, I truly believe the Lord will answer our prayers, our children will be saved and they will return to Him. Sometimes it's the so-called prodigal child who becomes the strongest Christian of all. I have seen that happen many times.

The Name Above All Names

"Also I say to you, whoever confesses Me before men, him the Son of Man also will confess before the angels of God. But he who denies Me before men will be denied before the angels of God."

~ Luke 12:8-9

When speaking to large crowds, I usually get a clear reaction or response when I mention the name of Jesus Christ. Sometimes it's volatile or sarcastic. People will say to me, "How can you say that there is only one God? How can you say that there is no other way to Heaven?" Yet, Jesus clearly says in John 14:6 "I am the way, the truth, and the life. No one comes to the Father except through Me."

The other response I get is from people who have found hope in the Name above all names; the love that they've sought after was found in God. Because He is love. They found a Friend who sticks closer than a brother. They found a reason for living, because they found the Son of God.

Today, I encourage you to call on the Name of our Lord Jesus Christ. It is through Jesus Christ that we have access to our Heavenly Father and are in fellowship with the Holy Spirit daily. What a wonderful Name it is, the Name of Jesus Christ our King.

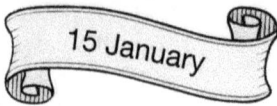

Know Him More Intimately

Those who know Your name will put their trust in You; for You, LORD, have not forsaken those who seek You. Sing praises to the LORD, who dwells in Zion! Declare His deeds among the people.

~ Psalm 9:10-11

If I had the opportunity to live my life over again and to pursue any career, my greatest desire would be to know Jesus more intimately. I would've saved myself from so many trials and unnecessary pain if only I had known my Saviour then like I do now.

The strength and fortitude that one receives when putting your ultimate trust, hope and faith in Jesus Christ are just amazing. He literally changes a worm into a butterfly. He takes away fear and gives purpose and meaning to our lives.

Often after an event where millions of people gathered to worship God and experience the presence of the Holy Spirit, people will approach us and say, "What amazing things you have done!" I'll just answer, "No, it was not us; it was God." God worked in us. It is all His doing.

I am living my dream and doing things that I would never have attempted before I met Jesus Christ. To Him be all the praise, honour and glory.

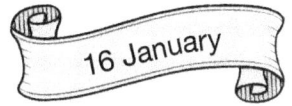

Times of Tribulation

And not only that, but we also glory in tribulations, knowing that tribulation produces perseverance; and perseverance, character; and character, hope.

~ Romans 5:3-4

Have you ever wondered why you have to go through hardship? I have wondered about that many times in the past, especially as a young farmer.

My training ground was agriculture. We have grown many different crops, from potatoes to maize, beans, tomatoes and cabbage. We have farmed with chickens, pigs, sheep, cattle and horses. In each of those different categories the Lord has taught me many lessons. Probably the greatest lesson I have learned through farming is patience. By nature I am an impulsive person and I want to get on and do things, but nature has taught me to be patient.

When I was young, I did some agricultural training in Scotland. During this time, I went through a muddy patch on a flat piece of ground with a tractor and got stuck. I tried everything I could and eventually turned off the engine. The supervisor got in the tractor, switched the engine on and used the four-wheel drive option. He drove the tractor straight out.

The moral of the story is that if we just take time and look at the complete picture, be patient and calm, we will save ourselves a lot of trouble.

Your Choice

As for me and my house, we will serve the LORD.

~ Joshua 24:15

Life is full of choices and we shouldn't judge people who make the wrong ones, because those who live in glass houses should not throw stones. However, there are always consequences for bad decisions. It saddens me to hear of many great men and women of God who have made bad choices and all their hard work to build up their ministry collapsed in an instant.

We cannot use the excuse, "Well, the devil caught me and I was powerless to stand against him," because in 1 John 4:4 Jesus says, "He who is in you is greater than he who is in the world." The truth is we made a choice and if it was a bad one, the first thing we need to do is to stop, repent, ask forgiveness from the Lord and turn back to Him.

There is one of two routes to pick – the right way or the wrong way. The choice is ours, but we are still going to stand before the Lord on the Day of Judgement. The right way is to obey God, to walk according to His statutes and to love Him and others with all our hearts.

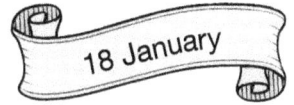

Settle Your Differences

"Why can't you decide for yourselves what is right? When you are on the way to court with your accuser, try to settle the matter before you get there. Otherwise, your accuser may drag you before the judge, who will hand you over to an officer, who will throw you into prison. And if that happens, you won't be free again until you have paid the very last penny."

~ Luke 12:57-59 NLT

It is a tragedy that believers cannot settle their differences out of court. We need to settle the differences between each other and before the Lord. The best and the fairest judgement is always the Word of God. We need to trust the council of the written Word of God to settle our differences.

Money is too often the root cause of conflict. I know people who have had lifelong friendships and right at the end of their lives became business partners only to end up as arch-enemies all because of money.

Do not seek the counsel of men at a great financial cost when the counsel of God is available for free. The Bible is black and white, crystal clear, simple and always works. Ask God to guide you with His Word as you and your fellow believers try to see eye-to-eye again.

Tears of Joy

Those who sow in tears shall reap in joy. He who continually goes forth weeping, bearing seed for sowing, shall doubtless come again with rejoicing, bringing his sheaves with him.

~ Psalm 126:5-6

Some of us have sowed seeds our whole lives and we haven't seen much harvest for it. As a farmer, I can tell you that no seed will germinate without moisture. If you keep seed dry in a shed, it will stay like that for years. But if you plant it in a field with moisture, it will germinate and it will bear a mighty crop.

Those who have sown good seeds, the Word of God, will definitely reap a mighty crop. Maybe not now, but you will hear about it in Heaven one day. We have an obligation to tell people with compassion and love that they need to be born again.

We are to preach the Gospel of Jesus Christ in season and out of season, and not only when we feel like it. It's not about us, it's all about Jesus. All we have to do is sow the seeds and Jesus will make them grow. He brings in a bountiful harvest.

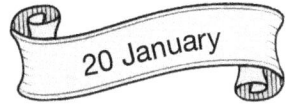

Decision Time

Then another of His disciples said to Him, "Lord, let me first go and bury my father." But Jesus said to him, "Follow Me, and let the dead bury their own dead."
~ Matthew 8:21-22

I firmly believe that what Jesus meant is that we cannot wait any longer for those who are not willing to follow the Lord. We can pray for them, but they need to decide for themselves. We have a mission, a calling and an obligation.

Jesus says to us in Mark 16:15, "Go into all the world and preach the Gospel to every creature." We need to do this with passion and complete surrender to God. There is an old saying, "The road to hell is paved with good intentions." We need to start doing what God has called us to and not just speak about it.

There are many different ways to preach the Gospel – in the workplace, on the sports field, in hospital, in prison or in the church – but we really need to be intentional with everyone around us and in every place we find ourselves. It is decision time!

Once you have committed yourself completely to Him, peace that surpasses all understanding will fill you as you do what the Lord has told you to do.

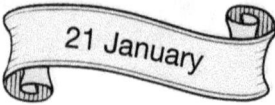

Remember Your Conduct

Therefore, brethren, stand fast and hold the traditions which you were taught, whether by word or our epistle.

~ 2 Thessalonians 2:15

In this day and age, we seem to easily forget the basics of living a good life. We need to get back to grassroots.

In 2 Thessalonians 2, Paul says that even though he was treated unfairly, he still kept the faith. He endured conflict, yet he continued to obey God rather than man. Our conduct must be a reflection of the confidence that we have in Christ and not in trying to find favour with other people.

We also need to speak the truth in love and not use flattering words, only to realise later on that what we said in our attempt to impress others was not the truth. That is poor conduct. Remember our reward comes from God and from Him alone. We don't seek glory or recognition from man. We need to learn to be more gentle and gracious with people.

A good reputation is worth more than money in the bank and we need to work at it. Once people know that they can trust you, they will give you as much grace as you require.

May God bless you as you remember your conduct, no matter who you are.

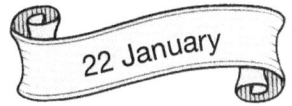

Beware of Neglect

A little sleep, a little slumber, a little folding of the hands to sleep – so shall your poverty come on you like a prowler, and your need like an armed man.

~ Proverbs 6:10-11

We tend to cut corners when the heat is on. For example, when we get very busy, instead of spending more time with the Lord, we tend to spend less time with Him. That is the wrong way to go about it, because that is the beginning of a meltdown.

We need to watch out for the little foxes that spoil the vine (Song of Songs 2:15). Not having regular quiet times, not spending enough time with the family, and not reading the Word are things that slowly but surely creep into our lives and steal our joy. And eventually we end up in big trouble. If we look after the little things, then the big things will look after themselves.

We cannot afford to compromise God's Word. Remember to be generous to your fellow man, care for your family, and look after your business. Keep your relationships pure. If you've made a mistake or if you've spoken out of turn, go straight to that person and apologise immediately. Don't allow it to grow and get out of hand.

Look after the small things and the Lord Jesus will look after the big things.

Getting to Know Someone

"Have you not read ... 'For this reason a man shall leave his father and mother and be joined to his wife, and the two shall become one flesh'?"

~ Matthew 19:4-5

Many people have asked me, "How do you hear from God?" Others might say, "How is it that you have a special relationship with Jesus Christ and how do you hear the prompting of the Holy Spirit?"

The more you spend time with someone, the more you get to know that person. I have been married for well over 45 years and my wife, Jill, and I can sometimes sit in a crowded room and communicate with each other with a single look. I know when she is ready to go home, or whether she needs something to eat, or to drink because I know her so well and she knows me equally well. That comes by spending time together.

By taking time to be with the Lord, we get to know Him. In John 15:7 the Lord says, "If you abide in Me, and My words abide in you, you will ask what you desire, and it shall be done for you." It's not about merely hoping for the best. It is about hearing from God and understanding what He says. He will confirm it through Scriptures.

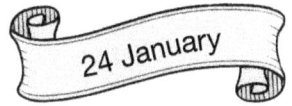

Purpose in Life

Where there is no vision, the people perish ...

~ Proverbs 29:18 KJV

Ask yourself a serious question: Do you have a purpose in life?

When I left Zambia in 1976, I was a young man in my twenties and all I wanted to do was to have my own farm in South Africa. I thought that would bring purpose to my life.

I have a beautiful wife, five children and many wonderful grandchildren. I got the beautiful farm that I wanted. But back then, even though I had all the things I wanted, I still had no purpose for living, no peace and no assurance. I was not sure that I would go to Heaven if I died.

I was working 16-18 hours a day and thought that if I could achieve my goal then I would have purpose. Then one day I received a Scripture from God that says, "Do not be afraid, but speak, and do not keep silent" (Acts 18:9). That was the light switch that came on in my life and I started preaching the Gospel.

Discover your purpose and passion in life. All you have to do is ask the Lord Jesus Christ to reveal it to you and then pursue it with all your heart.

Iron Sharpens Iron

As iron sharpens iron, so a man sharpens the countenance of his friend.

~ Proverbs 27:17

As a farmer, I never go out to work without carrying my knife with me. Without it I could run into trouble. For example, I could be riding my horse, Snowy, and he could get caught in some bailing twine in the field. Then I could jump off and cut him free quickly. There could be a water pipe that burst out in the field and I could possibly fix it if I had my knife. A knife, especially a razor sharp one, is absolutely critical to a farmer.

According to Proverbs 27:17, we need to continue to sharpen each other. Just like I use an oil stone to sharpen my knife, so I need a brother in Christ to keep me encouraged, to sharpen me when I am making a mistake that is not bringing glory to God. I need someone who can take the rough edges off and put back that sharp cutting edge on my life.

We as Christians need to keep ourselves mentally and spiritually sharp. We need to spend time in the Word, in prayer and in fellowship with each other. Make a decision today to keep your knife sharp.

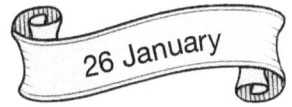

Nip it in the Bud

If we confess our sins, He is faithful and just to forgive us our sins and to cleanse us from all unrighteousness.

~ 1 John 1:9

God doesn't want us to hold grudges, or to persist with any kind of sin in our lives. Confess it straightaway and put an end to it. Literally nip it in the bud.

If we deal with sin straightaway, then it cannot grow roots. The Bible tells us in Hebrews 12:14-15, "Pursue peace with all people, and holiness, without which no one will see the Lord: looking carefully lest anyone fall short of the grace of God; lest any root of bitterness springing up cause trouble, and by this many become defiled."

Be careful of the roots growing in your life, like criticism, pride, dishonesty, lying and being judgemental. These roots, if they are allowed to become established, are difficult to take out.

But if we deal with them immediately and ask the Holy Spirit to show us the areas in our lives that need to change, then it is so much easier to move forward victoriously as a Christian.

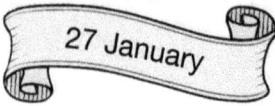

Waiting on the Lord

The LORD is good to those who wait for Him, to the soul who seeks Him. It is good that one should hope and wait quietly for the salvation of the LORD.

~ Lamentations 3:25-26

In this day and age where everything is done at double speed it is unusual for people to come aside and wait on the Lord. Everything is done fast – fast food, fast internet, cars, phones, etc.

The Lord has been very specific in the Bible where He says that it is good for us to wait for Him and we should hope and wait quietly for His salvation. People are so stressed and busy that the Lord has very little, if any time, to speak to anyone.

We need to spend more time in prayer. We need to come aside and wait on the Lord. If we sit down and count the cost, as Jesus said, before we build a house, then we will not build it in vain.

The Lord Jesus was never in a hurry and He was never late; He was always on time and we need to follow His example and do the same.

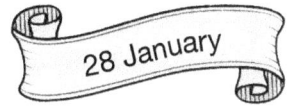

How Much Is Enough?

"Seek first the kingdom of God and His righteousness, and all these things shall be added to you."

~ Matthew 6:33

God has given me more than I need – He has truly blessed me. He has given me a wife who loves me, beautiful healthy children and grandchildren and, at my age, I still have my own horse. I'm riding my bicycle every day and I've got a reason to get up in the morning. What more do I need? But some people just never seem to have enough.

When you have Jesus, then enough can be very little. Some of the unhappiest people I have met are people who have so much that they are continually running around trying to make sure that nobody steals it from them. Some of the happiest people I've met have nothing, so they have nothing to protect and fear.

One of the biggest problems about having too much is trying to keep up with the Joneses. It has been the downfall of many people because you don't really need more. First Timothy 6:6 says, "Godliness with contentment is great gain." All you need is just enough.

Know Your Father

Now Hiram king of Tyre sent his servants to Solomon, because he heard that they had anointed him king in place of his father, for Hiram had always loved David.

~ 1 Kings 5:1

What a great start for a man when his father leaves behind a legacy of a good reputation. King Hiram of Tyre was prepared to give Solomon whatever he wanted because of his friendship and love for Solomon's father, King David.

People are greatly influenced by where they come from. Who your father is and your background history, influence your identity. I remember very distinctly when I had arrived in South Africa from Zambia over 40 years ago with a truck and trailer, a young wife, three babies and the fourth on the way. Friends were few and far between. People would come and visit, but not so much to help, although they did, but rather out of curiosity.

I want to challenge fathers to set a good platform for their sons and daughters to work from. There is nothing more beneficial than a father who leaves a good reputation for his children. And on the contrary it must be very hard for a young man to try and build on his father's empire if he had left a bad reputation behind.

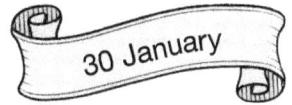

The Green-Eyed Monster

You want what you don't have, so you scheme and kill to get it. You are jealous of what others have, but you can't get it, so you fight and wage war to take it away from them. Yet you don't have what you want because you don't ask God for it.

~ James 4:2 NLT

If we read the story of King Saul and the young boy David, we will see very clearly how jealousy can poison a person's life.

Saul was a very handsome man; he stood head and shoulders above all the others. God appointed him through the prophet Samuel to be the first king of Israel. He had everything ... then a young shepherd boy came along and ruined it.

It is very important how we live our lives. We need to watch our hearts because jealously cannot only ruin a relationship, but a whole family as well. It is a blister on the heels of friendship.

That is why it is so important every day to start off with prayer, Scripture reading, and to hear from God. Lift your spouse, loved ones, and friends up before the Lord in prayer each day. That will keep jealousy and distraction from your relationships.

Affirm one another, see the best in each other and speak words that build up.

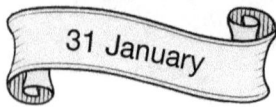

Be Kind to One Another

" ... For he loves our nation, and has built us a synagogue."
~ Luke 7:5

In Luke 7:1-5, we read about the story of the Roman centurion who was an unbeliever, and yet he was a kind man. The elders loved him. They asked Jesus to please help this man whose servant was sick. Kindness is something that stirs people's hearts.

Because of the kind action of the centurion towards the Jewish people, they rallied towards him when he was in need. Actions speak louder than words. I'm not saying that good works or kind deeds will get you to Heaven; you only get to Heaven through faith in Jesus.

However, James says that faith without works is dead and he continues, "Show me your faith without your works, and I will show you my faith by my works" (James 2:18). Because of the kind heart and faith of the Roman centurion, Jesus healed his servant instantly.

We need to live lives filled with kindness; lives that will draw people closer to Jesus. Let us exercise kindness and we will see what the Lord will do.

February

Let us therefore come boldly to the throne
of grace, that we may obtain mercy
and find grace to help in time of need.

~ Hebrews 4:16 ~

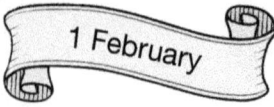

You Become
What You Think

The weapons of our warfare are not carnal, but mighty in God for pulling down strongholds, casting down arguments and every high thing that exalts itself against the knowledge of God, bringing every thought into captivity to the obedience of Christ.

~ 2 Corinthians 10:4-5

People are suffering. And much of the suffering we experience originates from our thought life. Be careful not to allow vain imaginations to dominate your life. For example, no good will come from saying things like: I'm not good enough; I'll never make it; I'm not up to standard; I'll never qualify. These are lies from the devil.

Paul says that the weapons we use to fight these things are not physical ones. The mind is the battle field. What you think is what you will eventually become.

The best way to combat the lies of the devil is to use the weapons that God has given us, that is the armour of God: the helmet of salvation, the breastplate of righteousness, the belt of truth, the shoes of the Gospel of peace, the shield of faith and the sword of the Spirit, which is the Word of God.

When we put those on every day, we will find that the devil is unable to attack us.

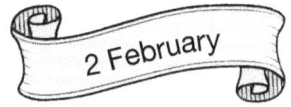

Pray Together – Stay Together

"For where two or three are gathered together in My name, I am there in the midst of them."

~ Matthew 18:20

One Sunday afternoon, my son had to bring a large herd of cattle in from an outlying field. He was short-staffed that day, so he asked me to help him with my horse, Snowy.

As I saddled up my horse, I saw one of my small grandsons, Josiah, being mounted on his own horse for his first out-ride by himself. The massive horse with this little fellow on its back was a picture that touched me deeply. My son was so proud of him! The three of us went out together into the field and brought in a large herd of cattle.

The Lord laid on my heart again:

- the importance of family
- that a family that prays together stays together, and
- the importance of teamwork.

If we can get this right in our country, we will see prosperity beyond our wildest dreams.

May God bless you as you continue to work on your relationships within your own family. And remember that praying together is the glue that keeps a family bound together.

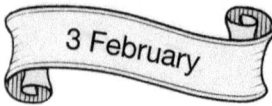

Relying on God

"Those who drink the water I give will never be thirsty again. It becomes a fresh, bubbling spring within them, giving them eternal life."

~ John 4:14 NLT

There are huge oak trees next to the dried-up brook on my farm. The brook is dry but the trees still bear beautiful green leaves. How is that possible? It is because their roots go right down into the ground, deep into the rich soil. Would the roots have gone that deep down into the soil if the brook always ran? No.

They reach deep down into the soil because these trees have withstood droughts before. These trees have experienced this brook go dry before.

They don't rely on the brook. They rely on the Creator and Provider, Jesus Christ.

Start doing things God's way. Not only will we find that the road that He has called us to walk in this life is not burdensome, but it will also become filled with joy and peace.

Get back to basics today – back to the grassroots of your faith – and start doing the things which God told you to do in the first place. Then you will find that all the things you have been struggling with will fall into place again.

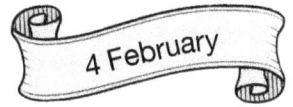

God's Will, Not Mine

Trust in the LORD with all your heart, and lean not on your own understanding; in all your ways acknowledge Him, and He shall direct your paths.

~ Proverbs 3:5-6

We need to seek God's heart for the plans for our lives and not our own. Jesus told us that He has plans for our lives, so we need to listen to Him and then do it. It will save us a lot of pain, suffering, wasted money and most of all, wasted relationships.

Let's get back to God, trust in Him and He will reveal His perfect plan to us.

We are here to make a difference for Christ. This is our finest hour as Christians. When everybody else is ready to run, we stand firm. When everybody else is ready to make other plans, we stand firm in our faith. When everybody else leaves their faith behind, we thank God for the hope that we have in Jesus Christ.

When we say we are going to do something in the future, we must never forget to say, "God-willing." Because of God's grace toward us, we can trust that we will be here tomorrow. Instead of making our own plans, rather say, "Lord, if You are willing, we will go do this."

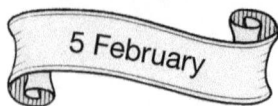

The Final Destination

"Whoever desires to save his life will lose it, but whoever loses his life for My sake will save it."

~ Luke 9:24

Jim Elliot, a dynamic and passionate young missionary, was called to the Amazon jungle along with four other missionary friends. They were called to preach the Gospel to the Auca tribe.

Jim Elliot and his friends were eventually murdered by the people they were trying to save. His wife and daughter and the young wives of the other men were left as widows.

There was a tremendous outcry throughout the world. Many people said, "What a waste of young lives." But as a result of what happened, the missionaries' wives and children went to the Auca to preach the Good News of Jesus Christ and many tribesmen were saved.

How are you running your race of life? Where are you headed and where will your final destination be? Make sure you run to win the prize of spending eternity in God's presence.

Jim Elliot said, "He is no fool who gives what he cannot keep to gain that which he cannot lose."

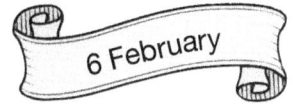

His Word in My Heart

"I am the LORD your God, who brought you out of the land of Egypt; open your mouth wide, and I will fill it."

~ Psalm 81:10

I am sitting quietly in my sanctuary, waiting on Jesus for the day which stretches out in front of me. There will be many challenges today with many decisions to be made, like every day. Some will be received well and others with resistance, or even anger. However, Jesus has assured me many times that He goes out before me and shall speak on my behalf.

I am compeled to preach the Good News because of the love I have for Jesus Christ, the Man from Galilee who has saved me from the depths of despair.

That is why I am prepared to leave the beauty and peacefulness of my farm behind. I am prepared to leave my family to travel across the mighty oceans to preach the Gospel all over the world. Jesus goes before me and I know that there will be a great harvest of souls.

I am doing what God has called me to do because I believe in Him and because, like Jeremiah says, "His word was in my heart like a burning fire shut up in my bones; I was weary of holding it back, and I could not" (Jer. 20:9).

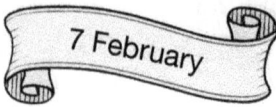

Waiting Patiently

God has made everything beautiful for its own time. He has
planted eternity in the human heart.

~ Ecclesiastes 3:11 NLT

If farming taught me anything, it is to wait. It is a discipline which is sadly lacking in society today.

We live in a time where everything is instant: drive-through meals, ATMs, cell phones and microwave cooking. Yet, if we want to realise our vision, the dream in our lives, we must learn to be patient. You see, every single drought ends with rain, and that is a fact, but we need to wait for the rain.

Maybe you are waiting to start a family or maybe you want to start your own business. Whether it is to graduate from university or to make the provincial sports team, you need to wait for God's perfect timing.

Abraham was a farmer and he learned to wait on God because he knew the Father would not disappoint him. In fact, he waited 100 years for his son, Isaac. God does not use impulsive people, He uses folks who will wait for Him.

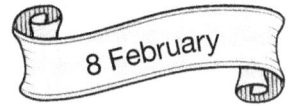

Believers Are Like Salt

"You are the salt of the earth; but if the salt loses its flavor, how shall it be seasoned? It is then good for nothing but to be thrown out and trampled underfoot by men."

~ Matthew 5:13

If ever the Church of Jesus Christ needs salty believers it is now.

How do we remain salty? It is quite simple: By spending time in the presence of God. By having regular quiet times each morning, you will never lose your spiritual flavour.

You see, if you and I live a compromised lifestyle, it will be impossible to have genuine quiet time with God each day. He is a holy God and He cannot and will not have communion with someone who persists in bending the rules!

So, in order to remain salty we need to spend time in the presence of the Lord. The only way that we can have a meaningful conversation with God is to repent of compromises made, and to obey His statutes, then we shall remain salty and full of flavour.

When you are among the people of this world, do they know who you are? Can they tell that you are the salt God designed you to be? Maybe it's time to go aside with the Lord and pray.

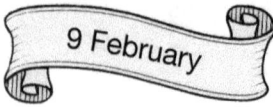

People of Godly Character

"Assuredly, I say to you, among those born of women there has not risen one greater than John the Baptist; but he who is least in the kingdom of heaven is greater than he."

~ Matthew 11:11

The world needs more John the Baptists today! Why, you may well ask? Simply because this world is in desperate need of leaders who lead by example.

Jesus called John the Baptist the greatest of men. The whole world stands aside for people who know where they are going. John the Baptist was not concerned about what people thought of Him. He had no fear of man, only fear of God.

God needs us to be men and women of godly character in these last days; men and women that the people in the world will aspire to be like. We must die so Christ can live within us. That's why the Lord Jesus Christ regarded John the Baptist so highly.

In fact, the Lord said there had never been a man born out of the womb of a woman who was greater than John the Baptist. He was the one who said, "He must increase, but I must decrease" (John 3:30). That's exactly what you and I have to do. We must be like John the Baptist. We should care less about ourselves and more about Jesus.

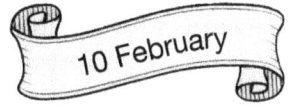

Cast Your Cares
Upon Jesus

"Therefore I say to you, do not worry about your life, what you will eat or what you will drink; nor about your body, what you will put on. Is not life more than food and the body more than clothing?"

~ Matthew 6:25

From one of my visits to Israel, I learned two very important lessons: first, to be thankful for every day that Jesus has given to us. Second, not to be worried about tomorrow, for tomorrow has enough worries of its own (see Matt. 6:34).

Those very special people, who have mastered the skill of not worrying about worldly things all the time, live life to the full. For they are only too well aware of the hard fact that anything could happen to them tomorrow! That kind of lifestyle is very beneficial to one's faith, because when you don't know what the future holds, you get to know the One who holds the future safely in His hands.

You'll often find that people who are content have been through the fires of life. They have learned that God is their Father and He will care for them as He cares for the lilies of the field and the birds in the sky.

So don't waste your time worrying, simply pray and trust in God.

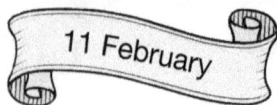

Learning from the Master

"For what will it profit a man if he gains the whole world, and loses his own soul?"

~ Mark 8:36

I like to spend time in the quietness of God's creation, especially in the African bush. When I'm there, I have time to reflect on the deeper things of life.

I was reminded that any learning, any move of God, must come from above; it cannot be learned at university or any educational institution. It only comes from time spent sitting at the feet of Jesus Christ.

That requires time and being alone in a solitary place. Without it, you will not be able to hear that still small voice in the midst of the frantic and busy world in which we live.

Choose to spend your time learning from the greatest Teacher of all time.

Thomas à Kempis said, "Far nobler is that learning that flows from above, from the divine outpouring, than that which is painfully acquired by the wit of man." In other words, spend time with God and He will teach you about the important things in life!

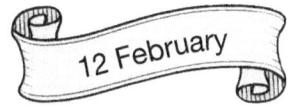

Birds of a Feather

"He who is not with Me is against Me, and he who does not gather with Me scatters abroad."

~ Matthew 12:30

We are associated with the company we keep. That is why it is very important to know the person whom you vouch for very well! Someone might give a person a job or opportunity based on your recommendation, thinking that if he is a friend of yours then he must be trustworthy.

You know the old adage that says "birds of a feather flock together". This is very true. People will judge you by the company you keep! It doesn't mean that as Christians we must not operate in the world … of course we must because that is where the harvest field is! But we must be very careful that we do not become like the world.

Let us make sure that we are keeping company with our greatest and best Friend of all – Jesus Christ. The greatest compliment that you'll ever get from any-one is when they can say to you, "I see that you've been walking with God." That comes by spending time with Him.

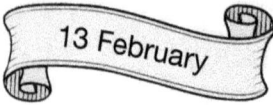

Use It or Lose It

"The kingdom of heaven is like a man traveling to a far country, who called his own servants ... to one he gave five talents, to another two, and to another one, to each according to his own ability."

~ Matthew 25:14-15

I was once sitting in the departure lounge at Oliver Tambo International Airport in Johannesburg, and a young waiter came to take my order. His name was Talent. I said to him, "You must have lots of talents with a name like that!"

He replied, looking very depressed, "No, Sir. I do not have any talents." I encouraged him and told him that God has given to each of us talents. This young man served us so well and that is a talent that not everyone in this world has.

Do not listen to the lies of the evil one. Father God has given talents to each one of us, but the big question is whether we will use them or not. If we do not use them, we lose them!

God then gives the talents we have not used to someone else who is already utilising his talents. And so, that person receives even more. This week, let us use the gifting God has blessed us with for His glory.

Stay the Course

Finally, my brethren, be strong in the Lord and in the power of His might.

~ Ephesians 6:10

I once had the privilege of spending a few days with some very special men that have asked me to mentor and father them.

During our time together we watched a classic war movie called *The Patriot*. What really struck my heart about the movie was a comment made by the general to his men. He told them, "Stay the course."

In other words, do not break rank in the face of the enemy, because that would cause certain defeat and would not only endanger your life, but also weaken the entire army.

Similarly, as believers and followers of Jesus, we are not to turn back, compromise, or stop fighting. We must stay the course. Don't throw in the towel.

By giving up, we weaken our brethren because, unbeknown to us, there are many who are watching what we do and say, and are affected by it in one way or the other!

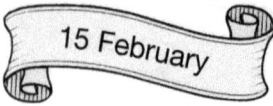

The Ten Commandments

"If you love Me, keep My commandments."

~ John 14:15

The Lord God our Father gave the Ten Commandments not for His own personal benefit, but for our own well-being on this earth. He gave them to us not to cause us pain, or to somehow spoil our freedom of expression or lifestyle. No, not at all! He gave them to you and me so that we might experience the blessings of an abundant life.

St. Augustine said, "Love God and do whatever you please: for the soul trained in love to God will do nothing to offend the One who is Beloved."

So, for our own good and well-being and for that of our loved ones, let us go out today and implement the mandate that Father God gave us. Then we will live victorious lives full of purpose and meaning.

In 1 John 5:3, the Lord says, "For this is the love of God, that we keep His commandments. And His commandments are not burdensome." His commandments are there to help us to walk this road without collapsing, without stopping, without coming apart at the seams and without breaking down.

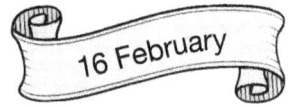

Never Compromise Your Faith

Blessed are the undefiled in the way, who walk in the law of the LORD! They also do no iniquity; they walk in His ways. You have commanded us to keep Your precepts diligently. Oh, that my ways were directed to keep Your statutes!
~ Psalm 119:1, 3-5

During my quiet time one morning, Jesus challenged me to never compromise His Holy Word. I try my best to walk in the Lord's laws, no matter where I am, or what I do.

I love speaking to young people because they want it straight, simple and truthful. In order to accomplish my task, I dare not compromise God's Holy Word. If I do, there will be no anointing and no power. In fact, the Holy Spirit will not be present at the meeting and for me that would be a nightmare.

If we are to see lives changed forever, healed and set free, then the truth has to be spoken, but always in love. Then we are sure to see the power of God manifest in a real way.

We all have a mandate from Jesus to bring light into darkness, to speak the truth in love so that the captives may be set free and people may experience true freedom in Christ.

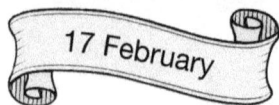

Be Still

For thus says the Lord GOD, the Holy One of Israel: "In returning and rest you shall be saved; in quietness and confidence shall be your strength."

~ Isaiah 30:15

The Lord has reminded me yet again that many of us are just too busy. We really need to start making Psalm 46:10 a reality in our lives: "Be still, and know that I am God."

Fear and anxiety are getting us down, because the devil is keeping us on the move. We don't spend enough time with God. So the things of the world become like mountains and we forget that all we need is faith the size of a mustard seed to tell that mountain to move.

I want to encourage you today to start taking time out to spend in the Lord's presence. Meditate on the things of God. Take time to sit down, become quiet and to wait on Him. Not to speak. Not even necessarily reading anything. But just to sit and to think on the things of God.

This time of silent meditation will change your life considerably. If you sit down and meditate on God, you will find that things will go much easier with a lot less effort.

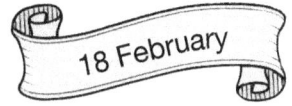

A Salute to Women

Husbands, love your wives.

~ Ephesians 5:25

My wife is my best friend. I thank God for her life every morning when I open my eyes.

In fact, Proverbs 18:22 states: "He who finds a wife finds a good thing, and obtains favor from the LORD."

When I sometimes ask women what they do for a living, they reply, "Oh, I'm just a housewife." I want to salute mothers and housewives everywhere; indeed you hold one of the key positions in society.

I think the role of a mother and housewife is one of the most honourable professions there is. I like to think that the Lord agrees! I say that because, quite simply, God trusted a young peasant girl, a rural housewife by the name of Mary, to look after His Son, our Saviour, Jesus Christ.

She was to teach Him, feed Him, love Him and raise Him to be the single greatest Influencer that this world has ever known. The Father chose a woman, a housewife, a mother. Not a group of professors, or a seminary, or a monastery. No, a regular everyday family.

Mothers, we salute you! We don't know what we would do without you. Stay strong and keep the faith. Your work will be rewarded.

Answers through Patience and Faith

Seek the LORD while He may be found, call upon Him while He is near.

~ Isaiah 55:6

As we are living in perilous times, many people are asking life-altering questions like: Do we go? Do we stay? Do we buy? Do we sell? Do we get married, or do we not? Do we have children, or is this world too volatile right now?

The answer is quite simple: Seek the Lord. Matthew 7:7 says, "Ask, and it will be given to you; seek, and you will find; knock, and it will be opened to you."

God is gracious. He will answer you as many times and give you as many confirmations as you need. Yet there are two things He requires from you. The first one is faith and the second one is patience.

I can assure you from experience that He will answer you. By the way, He might not always give you the answer that you want, but He will give you the right answer.

Sometimes the answer is "No" and sometimes the answer is "No comment," but it is still an answer. So, do not do anything until He tells you to.

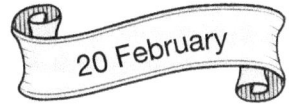

Don't Be Presumptuous

We should no longer be children, tossed to and fro and carried about with every wind of doctrine, by the trickery of men, in the cunning craftiness of deceitful plotting, but, speaking the truth in love, may grow up in all things into Him who is the head – Christ.

~ Ephesians 4:14-15

In this day and age where anything goes and liberality abounds, we need to be very clear about the things we stand for. You cannot defy the Word of God. We need to call sin by its name. Because there are so many young people who are confused. They do not know right from wrong anymore.

Young people are looking for answers. The answers are in the Bible and so we cannot compromise God's Word. The moment we do that, we lose the power, the anointing and the blessing on our lives.

So let us get back to basics, especially where it concerns our young people. Let us tell them (always in love) the truth, because Jesus Christ is the Truth (see John 17:17).

God bless you as you continue to direct people, not by your opinion or my opinion, but by God's Holy Word.

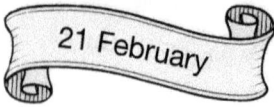

Walk by Faith

Now faith is the substance of things hoped for, the evidence of things not seen.

~ Hebrews 11:1

If you trust in your emotions you will never make sound decisions. Jesus said in 2 Corinthians 5:7, "For we walk by faith, not by sight." We cannot be guided by our emotions. This applies to young and old, male and female. We need to be led by God's opinion, not our own, nor that of anyone else.

If we are going to live by what other people think of us, we will never be happy. Only God's opinion of us matters.

Let's start hearing what God says about us. For example, in Philippians 4:13 God says that we can do all things through Christ who strengthens us. In Philippians 4:19 we read, "My God shall supply all your need according to His riches in glory by Christ Jesus." Then again, in Hebrews 13:5, God says, "I will never leave you nor forsake you."

Even as you are reading these Scripture verses, I pray that you can sense a joy, a peace, a hope coming over you. Stop reading the bad news and start reading the Good News and your emotions will become more settled. Your hope will be renewed.

Believe and Obey

Without faith it is impossible to please Him, for he who comes to God must believe that He is, and that He is a rewarder of those who diligently seek Him.

~ Hebrews 11:6

Without faith we will not make it and we definitely will not please God! If God is to work in our lives, He requires one thing from us and that is that we believe.

In Hebrew the word *listen* means the same as *obey*. When we do not listen to God, He cannot perform a miracle in our lives. In order to obey what Jesus tells us to do, we need to believe. When we listen to what God tells us to do, we will receive our miracle.

An example of this is the story of the leper Naaman in 2 Kings 5. When he obeyed (listened to) the prophet of God, Elisha, and went down to the River Jordan to wash himself seven times, God instantly healed him.

Start obeying the Word of God; that is what makes good soldiers of the cross. Then the world will sit up and say, "We want to be like you." Let us start to honour our fathers and mothers, to love our spouses, to respect our elders and to discipline our children. Let us listen, most of all, to God.

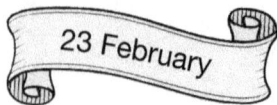

A Heavenly Game Plan

"For which of you, intending to build a tower, does not sit down first and count the cost, whether he has enough to finish it?"

~ Luke 14:28

Whenever you have to make a decision, count the cost. That is what Jesus tells us very clearly in the Gospels. Remember, the grass is not necessarily greener on the other side. Pray specifically before you change your game plan.

If in doubt, then don't. Anything done in haste is not necessarily from the Lord. In fact, the Lord is never early and never late, He is always on time. We just need to ask Him and stick to the plan.

When you pray to the Lord, be specific with your requests and supplications. It is also a good idea to seek godly council. Write your plan down and make it plain, so that others can help you run with it. Ultimately it is a faith walk, as is everything in life. Faith is getting a Word from God and putting it into practice.

Therefore, spend time with God and hear what the Word has to say. Seek godly council from elders, mentors and spiritual leaders, then make your decision. After that, don't ever look back. Follow through with the game plan and God will do the rest.

Our Good and Loving Father

Do not withhold Your tender mercies from me, O Lord; let Your lovingkindness and Your truth continually preserve me.

~ Psalm 40:11

My father was a big and strong man. He was a country blacksmith from Scotland and a great disciplinarian – he only spoke once and I responded immediately.

But he was also my hero. As a young boy, when we went out together, I always felt totally secure in his presence. He was always kind to me and concerned about my well-being.

God is our Heavenly Father. He is a holy God and not to be taken lightly. He loves us so much that He allowed His only begotten Son, Jesus Christ, to die a cruel death in order to save us from being lost for eternity (John 3:16). But Jehovah is also a consuming fire (Heb. 12:29) who will not accept sin or compromise from any of His children and He does it not for His sake, but for ours!

Ask the Holy Spirit to help you see the bigger picture and not to be rebellious and proud. Ask for a humble heart and remember that the Father disciplines His own because He loves us so much.

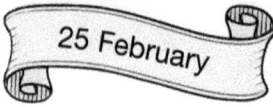

Faith Like the Centurion

The centurion answered and said, "Lord, I am not worthy that You should come under my roof. But only speak a word, and my servant will be healed."

~ Matthew 8:8

Jesus was amazed by the Roman officer's faith. He said that in all of Israel, He had not seen faith like that. Just like the Roman officer, let's start speaking out the Word of faith and let Jesus, the Miracle Worker, do the rest!

Nothing touches God's heart like when His children start to believe in Him and His promises.

If we believe, we step aside so that the Lord can do great and mighty things in our midst. He is not interested in good works. He's interested in our faith.

Exercise your faith today if you want to please God. Start to believe in His promises for you and your family, business, future and health. Then Jesus will step in and do exactly what He did for the centurion; He will solve the problem that you are burdened with.

Keep the words of Hebrews 11:6 in your heart today: "Without faith it is impossible to please Him, for he who comes to God must believe that He is, and that He is a rewarder of those who diligently seek Him."

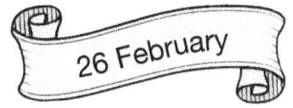

The Voice of God

If you are willing and obedient, you shall eat the good of the land.

~ Isaiah 1:19

Joseph, the husband of Jesus' mother, Mary, doesn't often get mentioned in the Bible. Yet he followed God's commands. For example, in Matthew 1:20, Joseph found his fiancé to be pregnant and was going to break off the engagement when an angel of God visited him. Joseph's obedience to God's instruction made it possible for the Son of Man to be born from the womb of Mary.

Again Joseph proved himself an obedient servant of God when he saved Jesus' life from certain death. He heeded the warning God's angel brought about Herod's brutal plan to kill Jesus and fled with Mary and Baby Jesus to Egypt (see Matt. 2:13-14).

We need to really seek God's divine guidance in our lives every day. During your early morning quiet times in God's presence, you will hear God speaking to you. Read the Bible systematically, pray sincerely and meditate on His Word. He will confirm your dreams, expectations and future.

Then have the faith and courage to follow through. Father God will not fail you!

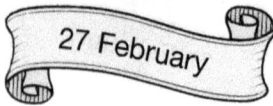

Confessing Sin

He who covers his sins will not prosper, but whoever confesses and forsakes them will have mercy.

~ Proverbs 28:13

Today's Scripture is simple and yet so profound. We need to stop covering up our sins. As long as we continue blaming other people for our problems and our sins, we will never prosper.

First John 1:9 says, "If we confess our sins, He is faithful and just to forgive us our sins and to cleanse us from all unrighteousness." Stop blaming others or circumstances and take ownership of your sins.

It's a human weakness to always try and get out of trouble by saying, "It wasn't me." We cannot expect the Lord Jesus to forgive us of our sins if we don't take responsibility.

In Proverbs we read that we need to depart from our sins once God has forgiven us and not continue in sin. If you have a drinking problem and the Lord delivered you from it, stay away from alcohol. We need to break away from relationships that have caused us to fall into sin.

You cannot continue on the same old ways. Our pardon is found only through the redemptive blood of Jesus Christ and Him alone.

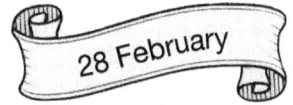

The Dew of Heaven

Therefore may God give you of the dew of heaven.

~ Genesis 27:28

There is nothing like the dew of Heaven to refresh you. You can do whatever you like and go wherever you want, but at the end of the day, it's only the presence of God coming down like morning dew that can refresh your thirsty soul.

That is why we read in the four Gospels that the disciples were often looking for the Saviour among the crowds. Then they would find Him up on the mountain, receiving the dew from Heaven. He was spending time with His Father, so that He could go down into the valleys to bless, heal and to set free.

The only way Jesus could do that was to receive refreshment and renewal from His Father in Heaven. First the mountain, then the ministry. You cannot minister to other people's needs if you have not received the dew from Heaven yourself.

Make a firm decision today to walk in the footsteps of Jesus Christ, to start spending more time with the Lord so that you too can go out into a world hungry and thirsty for God. You can heal, bind up, encourage the broken-hearted and give hope to those who need godly counsel.

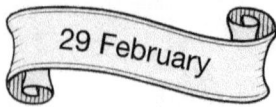

He's Not Heavy

A man who has friends must himself be friendly, but there is a friend who sticks closer than a brother.

~ Proverbs 18:24

I want to encourage you to look after your friendships and not to neglect them, nor take them for granted! We need each other, especially in the turbulent times we live in.

There was a beautiful song written many years ago based on an encounter that the songwriter had while walking down a dark, wet, cobbled street in London late one night. A small boy was carrying his baby brother on his back. The song writer stopped and offered to help, as he could clearly see the small boy was struggling with the weight on his back. But the little boy replied, "He ain't heavy, Sir, he's my brother."

We have to offer our help and support to each other much more than what we are doing. It's a commandment from God: "Beloved, if God so loved us, we also ought to love one another" (1 John 4:11).

Just a gentle word of encouragement, a small gesture, or a tiny lift of the burden, will do amazing things for the brethren.

March

*To each one of us grace was given
according to the measure of Christ's gift.*

~ Ephesians 4:7 ~

The Hand of God

"And it shall come to pass afterward that I will pour out My Spirit on all flesh; your sons and your daughters shall prophesy, your old men shall dream dreams, your young men shall see visions."

~ Joel 2:28

Do you believe in miracles, signs and wonders? I do! One morning, I was riding my bike on a quiet country road and speaking to Jesus (or more like crying out to God), asking Him to help us undertake a huge event that was coming up.

As I looked up into the early morning sky, in the clouds I saw the very distinct form of a massive hand. The palm of the hand was situated in the North and the fingers were stretched out towards the South, it was as if the Father was saying, "I have got this covered." The peace of God filled my soul instantly and I rode home rejoicing, knowing that Jesus was in complete control of the situation.

The great Christian writer C. S. Lewis said, "Do not attempt to water Christianity down. There must be no pretence that you can have it with the supernatural left out. So far as I can see Christianity is precisely the one religion from which the miraculous cannot be separated."

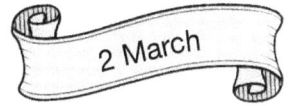

The Peace of Jesus

"Peace I leave with you, My peace I give to you; not as the world gives do I give to you. Let not your heart be troubled, neither let it be afraid."

~ John 14:27

One time, after a hectic but very successful campaign, I was relaxing in the bush, resting and observing God's beautiful creation. The Master often speaks to me through nature, probably because of my farming roots. The hustle and bustle of everyday life and the contrast of the peace of God in His beautiful creation is quite startling to say the least.

I observed a small herd of impala coming down to the edge of the water to drink ever so quietly, all in a straight line and not even disturbing the water. They didn't even cause a slight ripple in that pond … it was as if Jesus was saying to me, "Don't disturb the water."

We are believers in a world which seems to be running mad, where there is little peace and quiet, where everyone seems to be grabbing whatever they can for themselves, where it is a case of survival of the fittest.

Let our attitude be different to this dying world. Let us display that peace which Jesus talks about and bring the love of God to a desperate world.

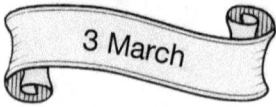

The Battle Is in the Mind

Do not be conformed to this world, but be transformed by the renewing of your mind, that you may prove what is that good and acceptable and perfect will of God.

~ Romans 12:2

A friend of mine sent me this message a while ago: "Make sure your worst enemy doesn't live between your own two ears." These are very profound words.

We need to protect our minds. Jesus tells us clearly in the Word of God that the weapons of our warfare are not carnal, but mighty in God for pulling down strongholds (see 2 Cor. 10:4).

God does not make junk so do not allow the devil or any of his representatives to accuse you of being a loser!

My favourite international rugby team is Fiji. Do you know why they have been one of the most successful sevens rugby teams in the world? Well, it's because they firmly believe what the Bible says about them. Furthermore, they apply it, believe it and physically wear it. Philippians 4:13 is printed on their jerseys: "I can do all things through Christ who strengthens me."

We need to focus on what God says about us and disregard the negative words the world has to say about us. Then, our whole outlook on life will change for good.

The Courage of Our Convictions

If God is for us, who can be against us?

~ Romans 8:31

Like never before in the history of the world, we need to stand up for the Gospel of Jesus Christ.

I have read the encouraging life story of Eric Liddell over and over. He was an athlete who was chosen to represent Great Britain in the 1924 Olympic Games that was held in France. Britain was sure to receive a gold medal when he was chosen to run in the 100m sprint.

But when he found out that his race was to be run on the Sunday, he withdrew because he firmly believed that the Lord would not be pleased with him if he ran on the Lord's Day.

Instead, he ran in the 400m race. The hand of God was upon him though … the valiant man not only won the gold medal, but also broke the world record that day. He said, "The secret of my success over the 400m is that I run the first 200m as fast as I can. Then, for the second 200m, with God's help I run faster."

Let's stand up for what we believe in, and Christ will stand up for us!

He Is Risen!

If the Spirit of Him who raised Jesus from the dead dwells in you, He who raised Christ from the dead will also give life to your mortal bodies through His Spirit who dwells in you. For as many as are led by the Spirit of God, these are sons of God.

~ Romans 8:11, 14

As we start this beautiful day together, let us do so in and through the "power of the Holy Spirit." Let us concentrate more on what Jesus requires of us daily and less on the demands of what the world (a ruthless master) requires of us.

Don't allow your feelings to control you. They can be like a roller coaster. One minute you feel on top of the world, the next you feel like you're down in the dumps. Job, who understood suffering when he lost everything (see Job 13), understood those feelings, as do many of us, but today our trust is in God alone. Second Corinthians 5:7 says, "We walk by faith, not by sight."

Today, irrespective of what is happening in the political arena, irrespective of what is happening on the home front, we know that our trust and our strength are in the Lord God.

We will then start to live in the fullness of the life God created us for in the first place.

Walk the Talk

A church leader is a manager of God's household, so he must live a blameless life.

~ Titus 1:7 NLT

We need to walk the talk. We cannot throw our toys out of the cot, as it were, and then expect to be used by Jesus as a leader in His household.

St. Francis of Assisi said, "Preach the Gospel at all times. When necessary, use words."

Sometimes when we have lost our temper, we try to justify our actions by saying, "I have rights!" But the bottom line is this: "I have been crucified with Christ; it is no longer I who live, but Christ lives in me" (Gal. 2:20). It is Jesus who lives in me and therefore I can't live as I please anymore.

The Lord is everything you need. But you have to believe this and live it, my friend. It's no use saying these words with your mouth but not believing it in your heart. You've got to walk the talk. You have to believe in the Lord Jesus Christ.

Let people see Jesus in you and want what you have – the love of Christ.

The Only Way

My old self has been crucified with Christ. It is no longer I who live, but Christ lives in me. So I live in this earthly body by trusting in the Son of God, who loved me and gave Himself for me.

~ Galatians 2:20 NLT

The way of the Cross is the only way to live in this world. Our biggest enemy in this world is self. That is why the Scripture says that it is in dying that we live.

Jesus said in Luke 14:27 (NLT), "If you do not carry your own cross and follow Me, you cannot be My disciple." Let us go out today and start to live for God and for others, not for ourselves. If we do, our lives will take on a completely new direction.

I once heard a story about a little boy who always complained to his mother that he didn't have shoes to wear. That is until he saw another little boy being pushed up the street in a wheelchair because he had no feet. From that day on, he never complained about having no shoes to wear.

It is when we take our eyes off ourselves and look with compassion and love at our fellow men that things will start to change for us.

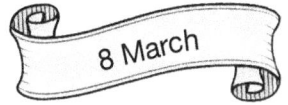

Guard the Faith

"Let your light so shine before men, that they may see your good works and glorify your Father in heaven."

~ Matthew 5:16

In 1 Timothy 6:20-21, the Lord Jesus tells us very clearly through His servant Paul that we are not to waste time with those who oppose us. Let's keep focusing on the important things in life and not tire ourselves out with negative conversation, because some people have actually wandered from the faith by following such foolishness!

In my many years farming, I have learned that actions speak louder than words. If you are running your farm in an honourable way, you don't have to speak much to gain respect.

Driving onto a man's farm, you will see first the condition of his livestock. When you get to his workshop, you will see the condition of his tractors, his tools. Then when you chat with his staff, they will tell you exactly what the farmer is really like. Like the farmer, when Christians model who they are, it speaks louder than words ever could.

You should always behave in such a manner that God's love can be seen in you. An easy way to test your actions is to ask yourself this question: Would it be acceptable to Jesus?

The In-Between Times

Without faith it is impossible to please Him, for he who comes to God must believe that He is, and that He is a rewarder of those who diligently seek Him.

~ Hebrews 11:6

Listening to a beautiful Christian song by Sandi Patty really touched my heart. She was singing about the in-between times and how we handle the days in our lives where nothing is really happening.

In other words, not the highs in our lives where everything is exciting, nor the low points where we are fighting the good fight, so to speak! But the dreary times in life when we have to persevere … that is where we need to be strong in faith.

Sometimes in the biographies of great and famous people, only the exciting and big moments in their lives are mentioned and not the years of preparation they had to go through to get there. It took Jesus thirty years before His ministry started! The in-between times are vital if we are going to be groomed to do great things for God.

Don't despise small beginnings and times of waiting in between.

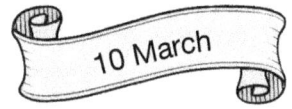

Find True Peace

When people commend themselves, it doesn't count for much. The important thing is for the Lord to commend them.

~ 2 Corinthians 10:18 NLT

True peace comes from finding approval from God alone. When we are concerned about what people think of us, we will never have peace and contentment in our hearts.

Simply because people are fickle: one day you are a hero and the next day a zero. If you do not believe me, just ask any prominent sportsman. If he has a great game, everybody idolises him … but if he has a poor game, those same fans want to crucify him! Thomas à Kempis put it beautifully: "He has great tranquillity of heart who cares neither for the praises nor the fault-finding of men."

John the Baptist did what God told him to do until the end; and as a result, he now rests in God's arms. King Herod, on the other hand, sought favour with man instead. He is now infamous in the eyes of history.

Let's start doing things God's way and put peer pressure behind us. God's favour is all we need.

The Inner Life

"These things I have spoken to you, that in Me you may have peace. In the world you will have tribulation; but be of good cheer, I have overcome the world."

~ John 16:33

True peace can only be found in the presence of God. Today's Scripture verse is more applicable now than ever before. We really need to live lives that please God and not people!

The more you try to please people, the more you will fail and the more you fail, the more unhappy you will become. We will never find peace and purpose while trying to make people happy and seeking acceptance from them.

We need to obey the commands of God alone by seeking our peace and acceptance from Him. Jesus Christ is the only One who died for the sins of people.

He showed His great love for us on the cross. That is why our quiet time is vitally important. In the presence of the One who loves and appreciates you more than anything in the world, is where you will find peace and contentment.

It is really not important what people's opinions are about you; what is very important is God's opinion about you, because He loves you and knows you better than anyone else.

When God Is For You

He who is in you is greater than he who is in the world.
~ 1 John 4:4

When we know who we are in Christ Jesus, then today's Scripture verse applies. Therefore if God is for you, there is no one who will be able to stand against you (see Rom. 8:31). The key to unlocking these incredible promises from God is found in a personal relationship with Him.

We need to get to know Him more. You might very well ask, "How?" The same way you get to know anybody else, by spending time with Him. Get up early in the morning and spend a good solid quiet time with Jesus – reading His Word, praying and meditating on Scripture.

If we feed ourselves garbage we will never have victory over evil, if we want to be used by God to achieve great things for Him we must only feed our minds and souls with God's Word.

However, if we spend time with God, believing what He says about us, operating in the power and love of the Holy Spirit that He has given to each one of us, then we will be more than conquerors (see Eph. 3:20).

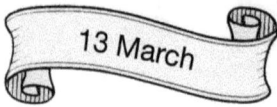

A Contrite Heart

The sacrifices of God are a broken spirit, a broken and a contrite heart – these, O God, You will not despise.

~ Psalm 51:17

Jesus is looking for a contrite heart. It is a heart that knows what it is like to mess up big time and then seeks God's forgiveness, which we receive because of the sacrifice Jesus made for sinners like you and me. Yes, our sin caused His death on the cross. But praise be to God that "if we confess our sins, He is faithful and just to forgive us our sin and to cleanse us from all unrighteousness" (1 John 1:9).

David, when he wrote Psalm 51, had just been exposed by the prophet Nathan. David had been caught in adultery with Bathsheba. He was broken and contrite in heart. His sin had cost him, but because this great man of God knew how to repent, God forgave him.

With a humble and contrite spirit, Father God will use you and me to bring many souls to Christ. People always open their hearts to someone who does not judge them, but who rather loves them!

Remember, it's not so much what you say, but rather who you are and the attitude of your heart that will change a person's life.

A Humble Spirit

We can make our plans, but the LORD determines our steps.
~ Proverbs 16:9 NLT

Thomas à Kempis said, "Man proposes, but God disposes." Yes, indeed we can make our plans, but the Lord determines our steps!

It can be very humbling when one thinks that through hard work and ingenuity you have achieved something of substance, when in fact it has been the work of the Heavenly Father all along. We can do nothing without Him. Do not be slow to give Jesus His due, because if we are to be brutally honest with ourselves, we are nowhere and can't achieve anything of real value without Him.

Humility is such a wonderful virtue for a man and woman of God to possess. Someone who displayed this virtue was Robert Murray M'Cheyne. God used him to start a mighty revival in Dundee, Scotland many years ago.

One of the things M'Cheyne said that has always stood out for me was, "I was but an adoring spectator rather than an instrument." This is so true. Let's not be slow today to acknowledge where all of our success comes from.

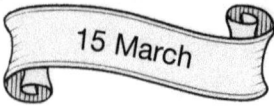

The Lord Gives Direction

He who observes the wind will not sow, and he who regards the clouds will not reap.

~ Ecclesiastes 11:4

We have been talking and praying much about the weather the last few years in our country and God has been, as always, so gracious to us. We need to continue to walk by faith and not by sight (see 2 Cor. 5:7). We need to seek the Lord for direction and not be governed by the weather.

If the Lord says we must plant, then we better plant. If the Lord says we must harvest, then we better harvest. When I look back on my farming life, there have been many times when I was directed by God to do things that, as a farmer, I thought were outrageous. Yet they saved the day for me financially and I learned to trust God rather than my instincts.

Listen for that small voice giving you direction, saying to you, "Your ears shall hear a word behind you, saying, 'This is the way, walk in it,' whenever you turn to the right hand or whenever you turn to the left" (Isa. 30:21). Let our yes be yes, and our no be no, and then with God, we will succeed.

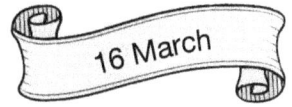

Blessed Rain

"While he was still a long way off, his father saw him coming. Filled with love and compassion, he ran to his son, embraced him, and kissed him."

~ Luke 15:20 NLT

A while ago God showed tremendous compassion and love for the farmers and townsfolk in the western part of South Africa. He prompted us to call an open, interdenominational prayer meeting, asking the Father to urgently send life-giving rain to the land, lest the people perish!

And what happened? Exactly what the Word said about the prodigal son. When his father saw the intentions of his wayward son returning home, he ran to him with so much love and gratitude.

I firmly believe that when Jesus saw His people come together to repent, to pray for mercy and to ask for rain, He sent the rain ahead of us. We went to this prayer meeting as representatives of the nation and prayed for forgiveness for the way in which we had disregarded God, just like the prodigal son did. We also thanked Him for the rain which had already fallen and asked Him to please sustain the rain so that the crops can grow to maturity.

We were met by the presence of our blessed Lord. He never disappoints His people who earnestly come to Him in prayer.

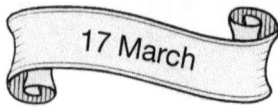

God's Way

Two are better than one, because they have a good reward for their labor. For if they fall, one will lift up his companion.

~ Ecclesiastes 4:9-10

As I grow older, I realise how much we need each other. No man is an island. Frank Sinatra sang a song called *My Way*. It is an incredibly sad song. Doing things his way on his own didn't help him at all, and such independence won't help me and you. We need each other!

Ecclesiastes 4:12 says, "A threefold cord is not quickly broken." Let us stand together and allow the Lord Jesus Christ to work through us. He said that when two or three are gathered together in His name, there He will be in the midst of them.

Especially in the Kingdom of God, there is no such thing as a lone ranger. We have to walk in unity.

Moses was wearing himself out solving the problems of the Israelites. Jethro told Moses to get help (see Exod. 18:17-23). He listened and it worked. God never expects us to be lone rangers. Take the support that is offered from fellow believers.

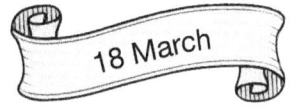

The Sacred Vow of Marriage

Marriage is honorable among all, and the bed undefiled.
~ Hebrews 13:4

One night, while I was listening to world news, my heart was very disturbed when I heard that yet another world leader had disregarded the sacredness of the marriage covenant. He cheated on his wife with another woman.

Most disturbing to me was that the majority of the public didn't care. Some time after the scandal, a poll was taken which showed that the public was unconcerned about what a president did in his private life, as long as he ran the country well.

We really need to guard our marriages, literally with our lives and educate our children about this God-instituted commitment!

It is not optional, it is until "death do us part." Respect the marriage covenant, put God at the centre of your relationship and you will live a happy life with your spouse.

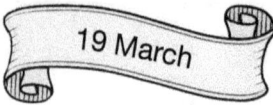

Trust God

Don't worry about anything; instead, pray about everything.
Tell God what you need, and thank Him for all He has done.

~ Philippians 4:6 NLT

At the beginning of the year there are always serious decisions to make. It's best to decide now whether you are going to go through this whole year worrying about everything, especially the future, or are you going to put your hope and trust in the living God?

If you continue to worry, the fruit of that worry will bring physical, mental and spiritual sickness to your life. It's believed that ninety percent of all doctor's visits are for stress-related problems, so you need to make a decision this year: Who are you going to trust?

Jesus tells us very clearly, "So don't worry about tomorrow, for tomorrow will bring its own worries. Today's trouble is enough for today" (Matt. 6:34 NLT).

The antidote for worry is faith and that is obtained quite simply by spending time each morning with God. Before going out to face the day, "give all your worries and cares to God, for He cares about you" (1 Pet. 5:7 NLT).

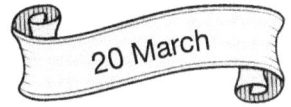

Ambassadors for Jesus

Christ in you, the hope of glory.

~ Colossians 1:27

Like never before in history, Father God is looking for men and women who will be the hands and feet of Jesus Christ to a fearful and confused world.

This is the most wonderful opportunity for us as His ambassadors to shine a light in the darkness, to be different and to be a friend to the lost, like Jesus was. St. Patrick prayed:

Christ with me,
Christ before me,
Christ behind me,
Christ in me,
Christ beneath me,
Christ above me,
Christ on my right,
Christ on my left,
Christ when I lie down,
Christ when I sit down,
Christ when I arise,
Christ in the heart of every man who thinks of me,
Christ in the mouth of everyone who speaks of me,
Christ in every eye that sees me,
Christ in every ear that hears me.

Let that be the response of every person who comes into contact with us today!

Godly Representative

Now then, we are ambassadors for Christ, as though God were pleading through us: we implore you on Christ's behalf, be reconciled to God.

~ 2 Corinthians 5:20

If ever God needed representatives here on earth it is now. Not compromisers, but genuine spokesmen for truth and righteousness. People desperately need help, counsel and most of all direction, because they are lost.

Jesus expects us to lead them home and not merely by our words, but more importantly by our example. To be an ambassador is to be a permanent representative in a foreign country. When people are lost, confused, misplaced or need help, as believers we should be ready to assist them. It could be just a smile, a pat on the back, a home cooked meal, an ear to listen, or a word of advice from the Bible. Just something to keep them going until they reach their final destination in Heaven.

Remember, we as God's children are foreigners here on earth. This place is not our permanent home. Our home is in Heaven. We are merely sojourners passing through. So, when God's people are stranded, we need to be ready to help them in any way possible.

What an incredible privilege to be counted an ambassador for the King of kings!

Be Kind

The fruit of the Spirit is love, joy, peace, longsuffering, kindness ...

~ Galatians 5:22

Jesus said that we shall be known by the fruit that we produce in our lives. An apple tree will produce apples, an orange tree will produce oranges. A fig tree will not produce thorns!

A kind word could just change someone's day. I remember clearly walking down the aisle towards the platform, about to speak to a large assembly of men. As I was walking, I felt prompted by the Holy Spirit to touch a man's shoulder sitting next to the aisle and say three kind words to Him: "God loves you."

I didn't see his face but just placed my hand on his shoulder and whispered the words in his ear.

About three months later we received a letter from one of his family members to say that he has since become a born-again believer, following Jesus and that his life was totally changed.

The interesting thing was that it was not the event, the music, or the preaching that changed his life, but it seems that it was the kind words I shared with him. His life was never the same again. Listen and obey when the Holy Spirit speaks to your heart.

Freedom from Self

Let nothing be done through selfish ambition or conceit, but in lowliness of mind let each esteem others better than himself.

~ Philippians 2:3

Self-centeredness is a big stumbling block to many people. The great apostle Paul battled with this. He actually talked to Jesus face to face when he was knocked off his horse on his way to Damascus to persecute the believers there. Yet he too, just like us, struggled with the flesh.

He says in Romans 7:19 that the good that he wanted to do, he didn't do; but the evil he did not want to do, that he practiced.

If you have been in despair lately because you feel that you are not winning the battle over the monster called "self," be of good cheer because there is a way out through Christ Jesus!

The same apostle said in the letter to the Galatians: "I have been crucified with Christ; it is no longer I who live, but Christ lives in me; and the life which I now live in the flesh I live by faith in the Son of God, who loved me and gave Himself for me" (Gal. 2:20).

Therefore, you and I should do exactly the same. If Christ lives within us, then there is no room for the flesh and we will have the victory.

Restrain Your Lips

Let no corrupt word proceed out of your mouth, but what is good for necessary edification, that it may impart grace to the hearers.

~ Ephesians 4:29

You know the saying: "Sticks and stones may break my bones, but words will never hurt me." In actual fact, this could not be further from the truth. Your physical body will heal, but negative and hurtful words can abide for a long time. In some cases it is only a prayer of faith and deliverance that can set a person free.

We need to be careful how we speak. Proverbs 10:19 says, "In the multitude of words sin is not lacking, but he who restrains his lips is wise."

If we cannot say anything kind about someone, let us rather not say anything at all. Encouraging words can make a big difference in someone's life who might be feeling lonely or rejected.

Today, let us make a decision to speak life and not death over people. Before we say something, let's ask ourselves a question: What would Jesus say?

Proverbs 16:24 says, "Pleasant words are like a honeycomb, sweetness to the soul and health to the bones." Let's speak words that build up and nourish others.

The Heart of the Home

"Behold, the virgin shall be with child, and bear a Son, and they shall call His name Immanuel," which is translated, "God with us."

~ Matthew 1:23

There are some people who call me a chauvinist. But that is very far from the truth. They ask me why we have conferences for men only and when are we going to host conferences for women? But they're missing the point completely. The conferences held for the men are actually for the benefit of the women!

We instruct men, teach them and pray for them in order to make them better husbands, fathers and to stand up as the prophet, priest and king in their own homes.

It was a young virgin by the name of Mary who "kissed the face of God." We salute women. Women have very courageous spirits: It was women that remained with Jesus when He was being crucified. The men ran away.

The man may be the head of the home, but the woman is definitely the heart of the home. Thank God for women. Where would we be without them? Abraham Lincoln said, "All that I am or ever hope to be, I owe to my angel mother."

Jesus Is the Living Word

In the beginning was the Word, and the Word was with God, and the Word was God.

~ John 1:1

As custodians of God's Holy Word, we need to be very diligent and careful not to fiddle with the Bible if we want God's blessings to be poured out on our lives.

Jesus stated in Matthew 5:18, "For assuredly, I say to you, till heaven and earth pass away, one jot or one tittle will by no means pass from the law till all is fulfilled."

If we want the power of God in our lives, we cannot compromise the Bible. If we want healing in our lives, we cannot doubt the Scriptures. If we want vision for our lives, we cannot question God's direction through His Word. If we want a blessed marriage and a peaceful home, we must apply the biblical rules.

Even the Master Himself, while being tempted by the devil in the wilderness, quoted undiluted Scripture and gained the victory (see Matt. 4:1-11).

If your friend says, "Show me this Jesus that you're talking about," then give him a Bible. First John 5:7 says, "For there are three that bear witness in heaven: the Father, the Word, and the Holy Spirit; and these three are one." Jesus is the Word.

Keep on Keeping On

Therefore we also, since we are surrounded by so great a cloud of witnesses, let us lay aside every weight, and the sin which so easily ensnares us, and let us run with endurance the race that is set before us.

~ Hebrews 12:1

Once, after watching the final day of the Tour de France, the Lord impressed upon me the importance of finishing strong. It is of no use starting the race with a big burst of strength and energy, but falling out halfway through. God is interested in good finishers of the race.

I am no expert in cycling races, but at that particular race the commentator said that the outright winner of the race was by no means a natural rider. So how does a very average rider manage to win one of the most difficult and famous cycling races in the world? Because of his steadfast, immovable spirit. He just didn't take no for an answer.

That is exactly what Paul talks about in 1 Corinthians 15:58. He tells us to be steadfast, immovable, always abounding in the work of the Lord, knowing that our labour in the Lord is not in vain. That is exactly how we must finish our race: strong, while serving Jesus to the end.

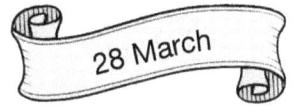

Doers of the Word

"Ask, and it will be given to you; seek, and you will find; knock, and it will be opened to you."

~ Matthew 7:7

I have meetings on a regular basis with about 100 men who have, over the years, asked me to mentor them and be their spiritual guide. This is one of the greatest honours of my life. They come from all over the world, different backgrounds, different cultures and age groups. But each of them has one thing in common – they want to spend time hearing and listening to the Word of God.

Early one morning, Jill reminded me once again that we have only one responsibility as believers and that is to make all people not just hearers, but doers of the Word (see James 1:22).

It was a great weight off my shoulders to know that those men do not really want to hear what I have to say, but they want to hear and do what God has to say in His Word.

At the end of the day, it is all about Jesus. Jeremiah 33:3 says, "Call to Me, and I will answer you, and show you great and mighty things, which you do not know."

A Consistent Lifestyle

Not that I have already attained, or am already perfected; but I press on, that I may lay hold of that for which Christ Jesus has also laid hold of me.

~ Philippians 3:12

Our world today needs more people of integrity and consistency in the way they live. Consistency is to be unchanging over time, not to live a life of contradictions, saying one thing and then doing something completely different. Inconsistency makes people feel very insecure, especially in a family.

I once saw an advert on TV that shows a grandfather and his grandson going out early every morning to catch fish. But every day they returned empty-handed.

All the other fishermen gave up along the way. A great storm hit one day and, after the storm had cleared, the fish came. The old man and the young boy were already out at sea and caught many fish! The next morning you see the roles reversed. The little boy was the first one up and went to wake up his granddad to go fishing.

Your children will learn to be consistent in their relationship with God if you are consistent in your lifestyle.

Make a Stand

Go, tell His disciples – and Peter – that He is going before
you into Galilee; there you will see Him, as He said to you.

~ Mark 16:7

Our God is the God of the universe. He is so big, so
magnificent, that He spoke one word and everything came into being in an instant!

Yet this amazing God of ours is also the God of every
individual. At Jesus' miraculous resurrection tomb, an
angel sent a message with the women to tell the disciples, including Peter, that Jesus would meet them
down in Galilee.

Why did he say, "and Peter"? Because Jesus knew that
Peter would never have come on his own after having
shamefully denied the Lord three times. That is why
I love the Master so much. He may be the Lord of the
universe, but He is also very much the Saviour of the
individual as well.

God can save you, too, if you will just trust Him. He
can make your business successful. He can turn your
marriage around. He can heal that sick child because He
is God. He is for us and not against us.

Truly Set Free

"Therefore if the Son makes you free, you shall be free indeed."

~ John 8:36

A friend of mine reminded me of this truth when I was a newly converted Christian: "Remember, without the crucifixion there could never have been a resurrection."

The crucifixion was the greatest act of love that has ever been performed in the history of this planet. As John 15:13 says, "Greater love has no one than this, than to lay down one's life for his friends."

Meditate on this Scripture verse today and think about the great sacrifice of the Cross. Confess your sins and God will forgive you and cleanse you from all unrighteousness (see 1 John 1:9).

Jesus died for sinners like you and me. Sometimes the hardest thing for believers to accept is the fact that their sins have been washed away by the blood Jesus shed on the cross of Calvary.

Once we can accept that, we don't have to justify our past actions. The only person we have to account to at the end of the day is the Lord Jesus Christ, because He alone is qualified to ask us what we did with what He gave us.

April

To Him who loved us and washed us from our sins in His own blood ... to Him be glory and dominion forever and ever. Amen.

~ Revelation 1:5-6 ~

The Goodness of God

"I will satiate the soul of the priests with abundance, and My people shall be satisfied with My goodness, says the LORD."

~ Jeremiah 31:14

My personal opinion is that the most outstanding sign of a believer, a follower of Jesus Christ, is the satisfaction that people see on their faces. This is what sets a Christian apart from those in the world.

The people of the world are very rarely satisfied – no matter how much they have, they always seem to want more. The opposite is the case with the follower of Jesus: Once they give their life to Christ, they are totally satisfied because God fulfils them.

The Lord gives His children unconditional love. We do not have to buy this love, or earn it. Jesus' love is given liberally and abundantly. In John 10:10, He says, "I have come that they may have life, and that they may have it more abundantly."

Let us sow the love of God around us and ensure people see not so much by what we say, but by our character that we are totally and completely satisfied with the fact that we belong to Jesus Christ.

Peace from Within

"I will make a covenant of peace with them, and cause wild beasts to cease from the land; and they will dwell safely in the wilderness and sleep in the woods."

~ Ezekiel 34:25

Some time ago, while spending time with Jesus, I received a very special reassurance from God that my peace and security is to be found totally in Him and not in my circumstances, where I live, or even my financial position.

This is wonderful news for the child of God – no more need for endless striving, for anxious moments, wondering what will become of one's little ones if we are no longer there. It is Jesus who is our ultimate peace and Source of complete protection, no matter where we might be.

He promises to give us His peace. He said, "Peace I leave with you; My peace I give you. I do not give to you as the world gives. Do not let your hearts be troubled and do not be afraid" (John 14:27 NIV).

Claim this promise today. Pray that Jesus will be your portion today, for His peace "transcends all understanding" (Phil. 4:7 NIV). He will give it to you in times of joy as well as in times of trouble. Choose to keep your eyes fixed on Jesus, the Prince of Peace.

God of the Whosoevers

"I say to you, her sins, which are many, are forgiven, for she loved much. But to whom little is forgiven, the same loves little."

~ Luke 7:47

We thank the Lord that He's interested in the masses, but that He also came for the individuals and the sinners like you and me. It is amazing how many times we see in the Bible that the Lord Jesus uses the whosoevers to do mighty works for Him.

Some of the worst reprobates have become some of the Lord's greatest ambassadors. Paul the apostle must be right at the top of the list. This was a man who dedicated his life to persecuting Christians, yet he became one of the greatest apostles in the Bible.

Then we have John Newton, who wrote the beautiful hymn *Amazing Grace*. He was a captain of a slave ship, a most unlikely candidate to be a preacher of the Gospel, yet he became a prolific hymn writer and a mighty witness for Jesus Christ.

Let us never disregard those whom we think are unimportant, uneducated or "lower" than we are. God uses people such as this to bring thousands to Christ.

Dream Your Dream

Whatever you do in word or deed, do all in the name of the Lord Jesus, giving thanks to God the Father through Him.

~ Colossians 3:17

Whatever your hand finds to do, do it! I used to dream about preaching ... well, most of you know my story. I used to preach to the corn, imagining they were people. Well, I'm not preaching to corn anymore; I'm preaching to people and I'm seeing a lot more people than the corn I used to preach to!

What about you? I want to encourage you to dream your dream. You know that God knows no limitations. Therefore let your heart run wild – get out there and do what He tells you to do.

It may seem that many people around us are going with the flow and we seem to be the only ones being different and swimming against the current as it were.

It seems ridiculous, but ultimately the Lord will vindicate us if we simply obey His commands. We seem to think that when the majority is going in one direction, that must be the right way, but of course it is not necessarily so. Use what God has given you where you are and dream a new dream for Him.

All Things ...

We know that all things work together for good to those who love God, to those who are the called according to His purpose.

~ Romans 8:28

When the Lord Jesus says all things, He means *all things*. Probably one of the greatest personal tragedies in my life was when my little nephew Alistair was on the tractor with me; we were driving along happily together when he accidentally slipped off. The tractor went over him and crushed his little body and he died in my arms on the way to hospital.

I cannot think of anything worse for anyone to endure. Truly, it was the darkest time of my life. But Jesus was closer to me during that time than He has ever been in my life. But the Scripture of Romans 8:28 is exactly what happened.

My brother, Alistair's father, has become a full-time preacher and is serving Jesus Christ with all his heart, as is his wife, Joanne. His eldest son Fraser is also working full-time for Jesus in America and his twin daughters love the Lord. Out of a horrific tragedy a whole family has been saved.

Even in times of difficulty and tragedy, remember that the Lord has a plan for good to those who love Him.

Put Your Trust in Him

Some trust in chariots and some in horses, but we trust in the name of the LORD our God.

~ Psalm 20:7 NIV

What brings absolute peace and tranquility into a person's heart is when their ultimate trust is in God. When I leave my wife to go overseas to preach the Gospel, I leave her totally in God's hands and I trust that the Lord will protect her, take care of her and see to her needs. She does exactly the same: she trusts the Lord to look after me and to bring me safely back home. Trust is an amazing thing – it brings peace, it avoids panic, anxiety and fear. We need to trust in the Lord.

I remember as a small boy, no matter where we went, I always felt safe as long as my dad was with me. I knew that my dad would look after me and he always did. That same trust we need to develop with our precious Lord and Saviour Jesus Christ. He will never leave us and He will never forsake us (see Heb. 13:5).

In biblical times, the shepherd would bring his sheep into the fold at night and sleep across the entrance. The sheep would be totally secure and at peace. That is exactly what Jesus does for us.

Clear of Blame

In the LORD all the descendants of Israel shall be justified, and shall glory.

~ Isaiah 45:25

I looked up the meaning of the word *vindication* in the dictionary. It describes someone who is clearly free of blame or suspicion. Jesus is our Vindicator; He is the One who clears us of all suspicion and blame. We don't even have to defend ourselves, because He will defend us.

Once we belong to Jesus, we do not have to continually give explanations of why we do things. He is our Vindicator and that is why I love Him so much. Whatever happens, as long as we do what God tells us to do, we do not have to continually try to explain ourselves.

As Christians, we can become isolated when we stand up for the Word of God. In fact, we will be regarded as the "offscouring" of the earth, the Bible tells us (see 1 Cor. 4:13), simply because we declare that there is no other god save the God of Abraham, Isaac and Jacob.

If we stick to our guns, the Lord will be our Vindicator. If we try to appease the crowds, we will fail miserably. Let us continue to do what God has told us to do and let Him do the rest.

Turn and Live

"I have no pleasure in the death of one who dies," says the LORD GOD. "Therefore turn and live!"

~ Ezekiel 18:32

The sheer finality of Heaven – or hell – is very startling, especially when a person dies, so much so that I believe this word from God was one of the main Scripture verses that motivated me to become an evangelist. I felt a calling to pluck lost souls from a potential grave of eternal damnation and to bring them into a living presence with Jesus forever and ever, where there is no more suffering and no more pain.

What the Lord is saying here is that He is very sad when a person refuses to change their ways and dies in sin, because after that there is no more hope for them. However, if that person turns from their wicked ways, repents of their sins (genuinely and not just to save their skin), they will be saved (see 2 Chron. 7:14).

Just look at the thief on the cross who said to Jesus moments before he died, "'Lord, remember me when You come into Your kingdom.' And Jesus said to Him, 'Assuredly, I say to you, today you will be with Me in Paradise'" (Luke 23:42-43). Remember, good people don't go to Heaven; believers do.

Faith Is a Choice!

"If you can believe, all things are possible to him who believes."

~ Mark 9:23

Faith is a choice, a decision to believe the promises of God, or to believe the lies of the devil. Recently, while I was having my quiet time, I read in Luke: "If you have faith as a mustard seed, you can say to this mulberry tree, 'Be pulled up by the roots and be planted in the sea,' and it would obey you" (Luke 17:6).

What holds God back from performing miracles in our lives? Quite simply, by choosing not to believe, it actually ties God's hands and becomes a great hindrance to God's miracle-working power in our lives.

Of course the greatest test for our faith is not when everything is going well, it is actually in times of crisis and testing, when everything appears to be going wrong. This is the time to proclaim God's holy and faithful promises over our lives: His written Word.

Not long ago I was kicked quite severely by my horse. I have subsequently suffered some severe pain. However, I have chosen to trust Jesus Christ to heal me. I have prayed for Jesus to heal me and I chose to believe that I am healed! Faith is not a feeling; it is a fact.

Believe in the Impossible

Without faith it is impossible to please Him, for he who comes to God must believe that He is, and that He is a rewarder of those who diligently seek Him.

~ Hebrews 11:6

I have often sat on the shores of lakes and thought about the Master walking across the water. It would have been impossible for a full-grown man to walk on water, but Jesus Christ walked right across the breadth of the Lake of Galilee.

Remember what Thomas said after the disciples had told him the Lord had risen, "Unless I see in His hands the print of the nails, and put my finger into the print of the nails, and put my hand into His side, I will not believe" (John 20:25).

Some time later, they were gathered together and suddenly Jesus stood in their midst. He never knocked on the door; He just appeared. Thomas fell to his knees and said, "My Lord and my God!" The Lord responded, "Thomas, because you have seen Me, you have believed. Blessed are those who have not seen and yet have believed" (John 20:28-29).

Let us continue to believe in the impossible, believe the Word of God and live in faith each and every day.

No Favourites

Then Peter replied, "I see very clearly that God shows no favoritism. In every nation He accepts those who fear Him and do what is right."

~ Acts 10:34-35 NLT

I always have a friendly argument with my dear wife, telling her that "God has favourites," to which she adamantly replies, "God has no favourites!" You know what: she is quite right.

Peter was invited to go to Cornelius's household, the home of a Gentile. When he arrived and saw how many people were there, he said, "You know how unlawful it is for a Jewish man to keep company with or go to one of another nation. But God has shown me that I should not call any man common or unclean" (Acts 10:28).

We thank the Lord Jesus Christ for the Bible, His Holy Word, which keeps us straight and instructs us on how we need to live. The Lord has no favourites and He challenges you and me not to judge another person; not to judge them because of their colour, their creed, their culture or their language, but to respect them as a creation of God.

Slave to God or Money?

"No one can serve two masters; for either he will hate the one and love the other, or else he will be loyal to the one and despise the other. You cannot serve God and mammon."

~ Matthew 6:24

When we try to appease both God and the world, we appease no one. I have seen it time and time again. The Lord says, "Blessed are the peacemakers" (Matt. 5:9). He does not say, "Blessed are the peace lovers." A peace lover will do anything to have peace. Such a person will often compromise to make peace, but it usually explodes in their face at some point.

We must be decision-makers as Christians. All roads do not lead home and it is not the work of a follower of Christ to be both a pleaser of man and a pleaser of God. We have to hear the voice of the Lord, get confirmation through His Word and then implement it.

I can tell you right now that we will not be popular with everyone. If you are a true follower of the Lord Jesus Christ, you don't have to try to be controversial because the Bible itself is totally controversial. Some of us, in order to be friends with the world, compromise the Bible. We cannot do that and expect to receive God's blessing.

The Saving Grace of Jesus

For all have sinned and fall short of the glory of God.

~ Romans 3:23

Early this morning while reading my agricultural manual, the Bible, I was again challenged when I read Ezekiel 18, particularly where the Lord talks about those who have blatantly committed sin. He says in verse 13, "He shall surely die; his blood shall be upon him."

I thought, *Lord, well, who then can be saved*? Then I read Romans 6:23, which says, "The wages of sin is death, but the gift of God is eternal life in Christ Jesus our Lord." What amazing news, what liberating news to hear that our sins have been forgiven.

Our Heavenly Father loves us so much that He sent His one and only Son to be the ultimate sacrifice for the sins of the world. Isn't that amazing? We know the story so well: we sing about it, we preach about it, we read about it and we pray about it. Yet every now and again the penny drops and the reality of the awesome gift of God strikes home.

It doesn't matter what we've done, it doesn't matter what we haven't done; the Lord Jesus Christ still loves us so much that He was prepared to lay down His life for you and me.

Enjoy the Journey

"You have sown much, and bring in little; You eat, but do not have enough; You drink, but you are not filled with drink; You clothe yourselves, but no one is warm; And he who earns wages, earns wages to put into a bag with holes."

~ Haggai 1:6

In the world today everything is speeding up. Many families don't even have time to sit down and have a meal together because everyone is rushing around. Often this is not just to make ends meet; it's for things that we want to buy but that we don't really need.

We need to understand that anything worth doing, anything worth having, anything worth accomplishing for God, will take time. What is required of us is perseverance, stamina and vision. We need to keep our eyes fixed on Jesus Christ; we need to follow through, we need to take our time and, most of all, we need to enjoy the journey.

At this point in my life, I am enjoying the journey immensely and I look forward to what's coming. Before we know it, one day we will be arriving at the celestial city. But until then, take it slowly, and be sure that you reach your destination in God's perfect timing.

Help One Another

Two are better than one, because they have a good reward for their labor. For if they fall, one will lift up his companion. But woe to him who is alone when he falls, for he has no one to help him up.

~ Ecclesiastes 4:9-10

We need to help each other and we need to be careful that we don't become too independent. Once this happens and we don't allow people to help us, we are going to get ourselves into trouble.

One thing that farming has taught me over the years is to be dependent on my neighbours. If there is a bushfire raging or someone's animal is sick, we help each other. Much more so in the church of Jesus Christ.

Don't wait for people to ask you to come and help them. If you see there is somebody who is struggling, go over and offer to help them. You don't have to preach to them – just love them.

Remember the two greatest commandments in the Bible are found in Matthew 22:37-39, which reads: "'You shall love the Lord your God with all your heart, with all your soul, and with all your mind.' This is the first and great commandment. And the second is like it: 'You shall love your neighbor as yourself.'"

A Father's Compassion

"And he arose and came to his father. But when he was still a great way off, his father saw him and had compassion, and ran and fell on his neck and kissed him."

~ Luke 15:20

What an incredible example of compassion we see in this parable. The father loved his son beyond all the evil his young son had committed and still showed him unconditional love.

Even after everything he had done, when the young man saw his foolishness, he admitted the mistakes he had made and decided to go home. He repented and his loving father looked past all of his son's foolish actions, joyfully declaring to his staff and family, "For this my son was dead and is alive again; he was lost and is found" (Luke 15:24).

That's exactly how Jesus feels about you and me. We too need to turn back and say sorry. Our compassionate Father is waiting with open arms to forgive us and love us unconditionally. First John 1:9 reminds us, "If we confess our sins, He is faithful and just to forgive us our sins and to cleanse us from all unrighteousness."

Getting It Right

It is eleven days' journey from Horeb by way of Mount Seir to Kadesh Barnea.

~ Deuteronomy 1:2

It was eleven days' journey south to the Promised Land, yet the children of Israel took 40 years to complete it. Why do you think this was? It was because they did not learn their lesson to do things God's way the first time.

We had a man working on our farm who used to build the most beautiful cattle fences. The interesting thing was that every time I drove past in my pickup, it seemed like he was making very little progress. However, his resulting fence was as straight as a ruler. He did his job and he did it immaculately the first time round.

Similarly, there are no shortcuts in the Kingdom of God. We need to do it God's way, or we don't do it at all. There is no compromise with the Lord. There is no second best with Him. If we do not get it right, we will have to go back and start again.

Did you know that, apart from Joshua and Caleb, not one of the original slaves released from Egypt entered into the land of Canaan? We must get it right the first time, otherwise the Lord will ensure that we go back until we learn.

A Delay Is Better Than a Disaster

Plans go wrong for lack of advice; many advisers bring success.

~ Proverbs 15:22 NLT

Be careful of spur-of-the-moment decisions – they usually don't work. We need to ask the Lord before we do something. We cannot do something and then expect Him to put His stamp of approval on it. It does not work like that.

All we need to do sometimes is to ask for advice, yet that thing called pride often gets in the way. We try and find the way ourselves, only to waste time and have to come right back to the beginning again. Rather take your time and do it properly the first time. When we ask God to give us an answer, sometimes He does not answer us immediately, but we must remember that there is always an answer. If God doesn't answer you, don't move until He tells you to.

Don't be afraid to ask a fellow Christian for their advice or recommendation. Then take it back to God in your quiet time, pray about it and wait for Him to answer.

The Gift of Self-Control

Giving all diligence, add to your faith virtue, to virtue knowledge, to knowledge self-control, to self-control perseverance, to perseverance godliness.

~ 2 Peter 1:5-6

People are under a lot of pressure, with the financial situation, with world politics, with the weather changing and sometimes we lose our self-control. This is unacceptable. As believers, we need to curb our tempers and control ourselves. Sometimes we say something in the heat of the moment, but once it is spoken, the words cannot be taken back.

There's the example of taking a pillow full of feathers out into a windy day, opening it and letting all the feathers blow away. You will never be able to retrieve them all to put them back into the pillow again. So it is with words. We need to exercise control over our tongues. Proverbs 10:19 reminds us, "In the multitude of words sin is not lacking, but he who restrains his lips is wise."

As Christians we need to do the right thing. Sometimes it is not easy to do the right thing, but at the end of the day, the Lord Jesus Christ will be very proud of us if we conduct ourselves according to the Word of God.

Know Who You Are

You are the body of Christ, and members individually.
~ 1 Corinthians 12:27

There is a story about a wealthy businessman who rushes up to the check-in counter and asks the assistant for his boarding pass. The young ticket assistant says, "Sir, I am terribly sorry, but the flight is now closed." The businessman, red in the face, thumps the counter and says to the young lady, "Do you know who I am?"

Turning on the intercom, she announces, "Attention, all passengers. There is a gentleman here who does not know who he is. Please could somebody help." It's a humorous story, but as we know, many a true word is said in jest.

As believers, we need to know where we are going, we need to have a definite game plan and, most of all, we need to know who we are.

Moses got off to a bad start in life when he murdered one of Pharaoh's slave drivers. Later though, after having met with God at the burning bush, he decided to obey God even though he was terrified. He finally knew who he was in God. We need to follow Moses' example and know exactly who we are in Christ.

The Lean Years and the Fat Years

He who gathers in summer is a wise son; He who sleeps in harvest is a son who causes shame.

~ Proverbs 10:5

In Genesis 41, we read how Joseph interpreted Pharaoh's dream about the lean years and the fat years. In the good years, Pharaoh stored surplus food. When the lean years came, not only was he able to feed his people in Egypt, but also many surrounding nations.

When God blesses us, we need to spend more time with Him and strengthen our inner man. We need to spend time in prayer, fasting and reading the Word of God, so that when the tests come in our lives, when the winds blow and the waves threaten to overwhelm us, we do not sink under the load. Instead, we remain strong in the Lord and thereby overcome the challenges that life throws at us.

Remember, there is no guarantee that we will have one bumper crop after another. We acknowledge that the Lord has given us strength to live this life on earth, but He has not taken us out of the fire. The acid test comes when the world watches to see how we handle times of testing. We need to ask Jesus to give us the strength, for to be forewarned is to be forearmed!

Show Your Gratitude

Since we are receiving a kingdom which cannot be shaken, let us have grace, by which we may serve God acceptably with reverence and godly fear.

~ Hebrews 12:28

As I sit in my prayer room and look out the window, the dams on our farm are bone dry. But I am not complaining because there is a gentle mist descending and I'm trusting the Lord that it is going to bring life-giving rain that we so desperately need.

If we look at the Gospel of Luke, chapter 17 tells us that Jesus met with 10 lepers. We read that Jesus healed all of them, but only one came back to say thank you. There was only one who was full of gratitude and love. Interestingly, he was not a Jew but a Samaritan.

We must stop grumbling because we don't get what we want. We need to start saying thank you to God a lot more for His blessings, because He is continually blessing us.

Maybe it is time we sat down and became mindful of the blessings God gives us. It is not a bad exercise to sit down with your loved ones and count your blessings, naming them one by one. You will be surprised at how good God has in fact been to you.

Integrity through Hardship

He who walks with integrity walks securely, but he who perverts his ways will become known.

~ Proverbs 10:9

When you and I as followers of Jesus Christ can walk the road of life without becoming contaminated (infected) by the sinful situation on this earth, then we can be satisfied. I read an article the other day written by the famous Scottish minister and hymn writer George Matheson, who wrote, "Canst thou walk in white through the stained thoroughfares of men? Canst thou touch the vile and polluted ones of earth and retain thy garments pure? Canst thou meet in contact with the sinful and be thyself undefiled? Then thou hast surpassed the flight of the eagle!"

If you can hold your head high when all accusations would come against you and not become critical; if people slander you and disrespect you for who you are and you can smile and forgive them; if you can keep your eyes focused on Jesus when you're going through the most hellish drought and your business is tested, costs are soaring and the currency is devaluing; if you can still be cheerful, then people will take note and turn round and say, "What is it that you have that I don't?" When you can do that, then you have surpassed the flight of the eagle.

Chewing the Cud

"Remember the Sabbath day, to keep it holy. Six days you shall labor and do all your work, but the seventh day is the Sabbath of the LORD your God. In it you shall do no work."

~ Exodus 20:8-10

Have you ever watched a cow grazing in a field? Normally she will graze early in the morning and she will eat as though it's the last meal she'll ever have. Then, after a couple of hours, she will lie down in the shade of a tree and regurgitate the grass she has consumed to chew the cud.

We need to take time to rest. Many of us run far too fast and as a result, life passes us by and is wasted because our programmes are too busy. Jesus Himself was aware of the need to draw aside. He spoke to His disciples in Mark 6:31, "'Come aside by yourselves to a deserted place and rest a while.' For there were many coming and going, and they did not even have time to eat."

I can almost hear you saying as you read this, "But I don't have time to rest." Allow me to remind you that even the Master Himself worked for six days and then rested on the seventh.

Let's not forget to keep the Sabbath holy.

The Company You Keep

Evil company corrupts good habits.

~ 1 Corinthians 15:33

I have heard such good reports about a few young men who are literally feeding the nation with their innovative and up-to-date farming methods. These young farmers are exceedingly optimistic about the future of their farms, their families and their country.

As someone once said, "Your mind is a powerful thing. When you fill it with positive thoughts, your life will start to change." We need to come alongside men and women who truly believe that there is a future for their lives, their families and their country.

Our Lord Jesus Christ is not a pessimist, He is an optimist. Just look at the Scripture in John 10:10 where the Bible tells us clearly, "The thief does not come except to steal, and to kill, and to destroy. I have come that they may have life, and that they may have it more abundantly."

Keep away from negative people, because all they will do is pull you down and undermine your progressive ideas and your vision, especially your God-given vision. Rather spend your time with people who will encourage and help you to achieve that vision.

Hard-Pressed but Not Crushed

We are hard-pressed on every side, yet not crushed; we are perplexed, but not in despair; persecuted, but not forsaken; struck down, but not destroyed.

~ 2 Corinthians 4:8-9

In Hebrews 13:5, the Lord tells us, "I will never leave you nor forsake you." Nowhere in the Bible does it say the Lord will take us out of the fire or flood. What He *does* do is to promise that He will always be with us.

No matter how hard it might be for you today, keep the faith. You might even feel that the Lord has abandoned you, but that assumption is not true. You must remind yourself that Jesus Christ loves you so much that He left His throne in Heaven and came down to earth to live the life of a mere mortal.

Jesus went through extreme hardships, the likes of which we will never be able to fully understand. He says He will be with us through the floods and the deep waters, through the fire, just as He was with Meshach, Shadrach and Abednego in the furnace.

We need to be encouraged. The heavier the load, the closer Jesus walks with you. Do not look to the left or to the right, or even behind you; keep going forward, together with Jesus your Saviour.

Knowing Him

"The ox knows its owner and the donkey its master's crib; but Israel does not know, My people do not consider."

~ Isaiah 1:3

You and I need to get to know the Lord Jesus Christ a lot more personally and intimately. We need to understand the way in which He works, the way in which He thinks and the way in which He acts.

When you get to know Him, you will learn what pleases Him, what displeases Him, what honours Him and what upsets Him. The best way to understand someone is to spend time with them. Spending time with Jesus is absolutely critical for a believer's growth.

When I travel, I try as much as possible to learn and understand the culture of the people to whom I'm going to preach. This is because you can easily offend people if you do not understand how their culture works and how they live.

This is a small thing but it is very important in building trust and relationships, especially with the Lord. If you know that it offends the Lord for you to serve other gods, then don't do it. If you know that the Lord wants you to be faithful to your spouse, don't let yourself be tempted. As we get to know the Lord more intimately, our relationship with Him will grow stronger.

The Boxer

"What will it profit a man if he gains the whole world, and loses his own soul? Or what will a man give in exchange for his soul?"

~ Mark 8:36-37

I was listening to an interview on a radio station recently about a former heavyweight boxing champion. I was quite surprised to hear that this big, strong man suffered from anxiety attacks, depression and stress. As a result, he had turned to alcohol and drugs. He was going downhill fast, even contemplating taking his own life at one point.

Here was a man who had made it right to the top of his field, yet it was worth nothing to him when he eventually received his champion's belt. The Scripture for today immediately came to mind. And that is clearly what happened to this poor man.

The good news is that some time later there was another interview. Every time the reporter asked him a question, he responded with the unadulterated Word of God. He had clearly met Jesus Christ.

There is nothing wrong with pursuing your dream, but it must never become the supreme purpose of your life. Jesus Christ has got to be foremost in your life, otherwise you will have a permanent void. Let us put Jesus first and everything else will follow.

The Sins of the Fathers

"Suppose that sinful son, in turn, has a son who sees his father's wickedness and decides against that kind of life. He … obeys all My regulations and decrees. Such a person will not die because of his father's sins; he will surely live."

~ Ezekiel 18:14, 17 NLT

Many a time I have met mighty men and women who came from disadvantaged backgrounds, who have even been abused or neglected. Then they met Jesus Christ and their lives were transformed. God is using them mightily as His vessels today.

We need to get away from the "woe is me" attitude and we need to start anew. Second Corinthians 5:17 declares, "If anyone is in Christ, he is a new creation; old things have passed away; behold, all things have become new." If you and I are new creations in Christ, we do not have to pay the penalties for our fathers' sins. So there is no point in trying to use your background as an excuse for where you are now.

We have got to put our past behind us and move forward. God promised that we will not be held liable for the sins of our fathers, therefore we have total liberty to move into and change the whole outlook of our future.

The Importance of Family

"Honor your father and mother," which is the first commandment with promise: "that it may be well with you and you may live long on the earth."

~ Ephesians 6:2-3

The family is such an integral part of the Christian's way of life. If we look at today's verse, we see the importance of the family unit in God's eyes. The Lord reminds us that children must obey their parents and honour their father and mother.

God expects us to work as a team. He tells husbands to love their wives just as Christ loved the church. He tells wives to submit to their husbands just as we do to the Lord (see Eph. 5:22-28).

Not too long ago, I watched the funeral of the late President George Herbert Walker Bush. He was a Christian and so too is his son, who gave a very touching eulogy.

What impressed me more than anything else was that nobody seemed to speak for very long about all his political exploits. Instead, each and every person spoke about the way he cared for and loved his wife and family.

At the end of the day, people are always interested in a believer's family.

May

*Return to the L*ORD *your God,*
for He is gracious and merciful,
slow to anger, and of great kindness.

~ Joel 2:13 ~

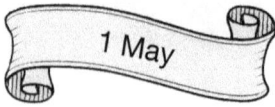

Inquiring of God

"Son of man, speak to the elders of Israel, and say to them, 'Thus says the Lord God: "Have you come to inquire of Me? As I live," says the Lord God, "I will not be inquired of by you."'"

~ Ezekiel 20:3

If we look at the words of God in today's verse, we see how indignant our Heavenly Father was when the elders of Israel came to Ezekiel wanting to question God. The Lord spoke to His prophet and you can hear by His comment to His servant that He was not impressed. His own creation had the audacity to demand answers from Him.

Such people have little idea of who God really is, because when we stand before Almighty God, we will stand with fear and trembling. I am sure that if Jesus Christ is not standing right next to us as our personal Lord and Saviour, we will fail to have the strength to even stand.

Let us come before Him, hat in hand as it were, and inquire of Almighty God with humility and awe. We need to love Him, respect Him and honour Him, for indeed He is an awesome God.

Loving Discipline

If you endure chastening, God deals with you as with sons;
for what son is there whom a father does not chasten? But
if you are without chastening, of which all have become
partakers, then you are illegitimate and not sons.

~ Hebrews 12:7-8

Many people do not believe that our Lord chastises
those He loves. Yet, if an earthly father, who loves
his son, disciplines him for his sake, then how much
more will our Father in Heaven, who loves us infinitely
and unconditionally, not discipline us for our sake?

The Lord does not chastise or discipline us because
He has an evil heart. On the contrary, He loves us so
much that He even gave His only begotten Son to die
for our sins on a cruel rugged cross (see John 3:16). God
disciplines those He loves.

We are not under law but under grace (see Rom. 6:14),
still that does not give us permission to live in sinful
ways like the world does.

There has got to be a change in order to acknowledge
that Jesus Christ has paid the ultimate price for our
sinful lives. Remember, God's holy correction is not to
condemn us but to save us from eternal damnation and
hell itself. Jesus disciplines us because He loves us.

With Privilege Comes Responsibility

If you remain completely silent at this time, relief and deliverance will arise for the Jews from another place, but you and your father's house will perish. Yet who knows whether you have come to the kingdom for such a time as this?

~ Esther 4:14-15

Edmund Burke once said, "The only thing necessary for the triumph of evil is for good men to do nothing." You and I, who know Jesus Christ as our personal Lord and Saviour, have a wonderful privilege, but with that privilege comes responsibility. We must speak the truth in love, for it is only truth that will set the captives free (see John 8:32).

We need to show by example how godly people should live. Husbands are to love their wives; wives need to submit to their husbands; children need to respect their elders; employers need to pay a fair day's wage for a fair day's work; employees need to work hard, as if they are working for the Lord Himself and not for people (see Eph. 5:22, 25; 1 Pet. 5:5; Col. 4:1; 3:23).

When we start to implement these basic principles, they will speak louder than words. As Christians, we have the potential in us through the power of the Holy Spirit to turn the world upside down.

Faithfulness and Honesty

"His lord said to him, 'Well done, good and faithful servant; you were faithful over a few things, I will make you ruler over many things. Enter into the joy of your lord.'"

~ Matthew 25:21

If there is one thing that the Lord Jesus Christ requires of you and me, it is that we would be faithful children of Him. When we are unfaithful, it hurts God, because He is never unfaithful. Second Timothy 2:13 confirms: "If we are faithless, He remains faithful; He cannot deny Himself."

The Lord wants to give His faithful servants greater responsibility. He is not looking for people of incredible natural giftings; He is looking for men and women whom He can trust and who are willing. I think anybody who has been let down by someone before understands how hurtful it is when a person is unfaithful. Obviously, we must forgive, but it is very hard to trust that person again. Let us be known as trustworthy and faithful; first and foremost to God and then to our fellow man.

Jesus Christ requires honesty and faithfulness from you and me. We need to be very careful of our lifestyle as we go about proclaiming the Gospel and living as His ambassadors on earth.

The Blessing of Mothers

Strength and honor are her clothing; she shall rejoice in time to come. She opens her mouth with wisdom, and on her tongue is the law of kindness. Her children rise up and call her blessed; her husband also, and he praises her.

~ Proverbs 31:25-26, 28

Today's devotion is dedicated to mothers. As I write this, I think of mine; that beautiful old Scottish lassie who was always so kind and compassionate to me. My mom was often not well, but whenever I got sick, she would sit up with me all night to comfort me.

Many of us are so busy that we sometimes forget our mothers. We need to be very careful and remember the fifth commandment, which states that we must honour our fathers and our mothers so that our days may be long in the land (see Deut. 5:16). This promise is conditional! If you neglect your mother, the Bible tells us that things will not go well for you.

I know that instinctively we love our mothers, but we need to tell them more often. We need to have that cup of tea with them and spend quality time with them. Honour your mother and appreciate every moment you have with her.

Overcoming Fear

For the weapons of our warfare are not carnal but mighty in God for pulling down strongholds.

~ 2 Corinthians 10:4

Our lives are filled with challenges and so often we allow fear, anxiety and stress (probably the greatest weapon at the devil's disposal) to derail us from being good Christians. There are forces that can paralyze a person: We wake up in the morning and hear that things are not going well; we turn on the news and find it is full of distressing stories. It might be nothing serious, but it makes one think the worst.

Most of the time, however, it is not as bad as we think. We have a choice to make and the battle that we fight is not in the heart but in the mind.

We need to take captive those negative thoughts and cast them far away from us. Most problems can be overcome, but when one starts to panic, one literally becomes paralyzed with fear.

The Lord reminds us in Philippians 4:6, "Be anxious for nothing, but in everything by prayer and supplication, with thanksgiving, let your requests be made known to God." Let us go and do just that!

A Fresh Perspective

I long to see you, that I may impart to you some spiritual gift, so that you may be established – that is, that I may be encouraged together with you by the mutual faith both of you and me.

~ Romans 1:11-12

Faith-building in our country is of the utmost importance at the moment. We are believing for new beginnings in our country, in our homes and in our lives, and it comes by speaking life not death.

It is so very important to come alongside positive people who believe in a new beginning, a new sunrise, a new day and a new hope for this country and indeed for our very lives. Accordingly, we need to keep away from negative people. It is so important, especially for young people, that they are surrounded by positive, faithful people who see the potential in the nation and in themselves.

One of my favourite Scriptures, which I find so encouraging, is found in Romans 8:11. It reads: "If the Spirit of Him who raised Jesus from the dead dwells in you, He who raised Christ from the dead will also give life to your mortal bodies through His Spirit who dwells in you." What a beautiful promise from Almighty God. We need to give the Holy Spirit lots of space in our lives, especially in our thinking.

Fathers and Sons

Train up a child in the way he should go, and when he is old he will not depart from it.

~ Proverbs 22:6

In this day and age where everyone is so busy and there is so much going on, it is easy to neglect our fathers. We need to remember to go and visit our fathers and to thank them for all they have given and done for us.

We need to thank God for our dads; they are our examples, even though they may sometimes drop the ball. We need to be understanding and forgiving and see a situation from their point of view. We especially need to extend grace as they grow older.

Celebrating our earthly fathers is a very important thing; yet the lack of fathers is one of the biggest problems in our country. There are many young men who do not have fathers. They have no mentors and they are desperate for a father figure in their lives.

I would encourage you, if you don't have a father of your own, adopt one. I am currently mentoring young men from all over the world and it is such a privilege and an honour for me. Fathers sometimes don't have to do anything more than just be there, to be a support and an encouragement to their sons.

Through Grace Alone

"I have loved you with an everlasting love; therefore with lovingkindness I have drawn you."

~ Jeremiah 31:3

We can never ever earn the right to be called the sons and daughters of the living God, or earn the right to eternal life with Him based on the good works that we have performed on this earth.

In Luke 17:7-10, Jesus uses a beautiful illustration so that we can better understand this principle: A servant is ploughing in the field, or looking after his master's sheep. When he comes in from the field, his master tells him to prepare a meal and serve it to his master. Then the servant may have his supper.

If the servant does all these things, should the master pay special attention to him for having done his job? No. When we have done the things God has commanded of us, we are still unprofitable servants because we have only done our duty and nothing more.

Everything that you and I will inherit one day is through the grace of the Lord Jesus Christ. Let us never fool ourselves into thinking that God owes us anything! Father God did it all when He paid for our sins by allowing His one and only Son to die a cruel death on the cross of Calvary.

The Lion of Judah

"If you indeed obey His voice and do all that I speak, then I will be an enemy to your enemies and an adversary to your adversaries."

~ Exodus 23:22

The Lord is telling us in today's verse that if we are on His side, we will have no enemy who can overcome us, because there is no enemy who can ever stand against the Creator of the universe.

Remember the story of the release of the Jews from Pharaoh's iron fist? In Exodus 14:13-14, the Lord says to the people through His servant Moses: "Do not be afraid. Stand still, and see the salvation of the LORD, which He will accomplish for you today. For the Egyptians whom you see today, you shall see again no more forever. The LORD will fight for you, and you shall hold your peace."

We don't have to fight; God is the one who will fight for us. What we need to do is to acknowledge Him as the only God and Saviour of our souls.

All you and I have to do is to allow the King of glory to defend us. He is more than willing and more than able to do so.

Storing Up Riches in Heaven

I saw that for all toil and every skillful work a man is envied by his neighbor. This also is vanity and grasping for the wind.
~ Ecclesiastes 4:4

Most people are motivated to be successful because they try and keep up with the Joneses and want to impress them. But this is meaningless, like chasing after the wind. We have got to be more focused and purpose-driven for Jesus and less motivated by competition, always trying to outdo our neighbours.

There is no time left on this earth for wasteful living. The Lord says to us in Ephesians 5:15-17, "See then that you walk circumspectly, not as fools but as wise, redeeming the time, because the days are evil. Therefore do not be unwise, but understand what the will of the Lord is."

We really do not have time left to keep going around in circles – like the Israelites did for 40 years – before we understand the will of God. John 16:7 tells us that the Lord Jesus Christ sent us His Holy Spirit. Therefore, we need simply seek godly counsel from Him.

From now on, let us start doing things with the right motivation, and not to gain riches on earth. Rather, we need to focus on building our wealth in Heaven.

No Going Back

Simon Peter said to them, "I am going fishing." They said to him, "We are going with you also." They went out and immediately got into the boat, and that night they caught nothing.

~ John 21:3

If we look at the incident that took place after the resurrection of Jesus Christ, we see that the disciples became very despondent – everything they had dreamed of seemed to have come to nothing (not unlike the way some of us feel at the moment).

Nonetheless, there is no going back. We need to press on by faith. Remember Hebrews 11:1, "Now faith is the substance of things hoped for, the evidence of things not seen." If we are going to succeed, we cannot afford to go backwards.

Peter and the disciples went backwards when they returned to the only thing they knew how to do well after the death of Jesus and that was fishing. But though they fished all night, they caught nothing.

Early the morning Jesus stood on the shore and instructed them to "cast the net on the right side" (John 21:6). They did this and caught a multitude of fish!

This miracle happened because of obedience. When Jesus undertakes for us, miracles do indeed happen. We need to keep moving forward, looking ahead and staying focused on Jesus.

Our Only Hope Is Love

Love never fails ... Now abide faith, hope, love, these three;
but the greatest of these is love.

~ 1 Corinthians 13:8, 13

One of the most well-known chapters in the Bible is 1 Corinthians 13 – the chapter of love. You and I know that "love will cover a multitude of sins" (1 Pet. 4:8), and therefore, as followers of Jesus Christ, we must get it right. We need to exercise love in everything we do.

The famous American evangelist Dwight L. Moody said, "A doctor can be a great doctor without loving his patients. A lawyer can be a great lawyer without loving his clients. A geologist could be a good geologist without loving science. But nobody can be a good Christian without love." I would like to add to that: A husband cannot be a great husband or a great father without love.

We need to ask the Lord to give us more understanding, patience and humility. We need to stop being so puffed up and move on with our lives in this world. Let us not look backwards, because love keeps no account of wrongs (see 1 Cor. 13:5).

As we stretch out our hands towards others, the Lord will honour that gesture and bless us with forgiveness, hope and love. Remember, God *is* love (see 1 John 4:16)!

Happiness Cannot Be Bought

I know that nothing is better for them than to rejoice, and to do good in their lives, and also that every man should eat and drink and enjoy the good of all his labor – it is the gift of God.

~ Ecclesiastes 3:12-13

My late father used to tell me and my younger brother when we were growing up, "If you ever get up in the morning and you do not feel like going to work, change your job." If you think about it, we spend most of our time at work.

There is a lot more to life than just making money. Of course we have to put bread on the table, feed, educate and clothe our families. We must also be responsible citizens and contribute to the furtherance of our beautiful country.

However, it will only all come together once we have found true happiness. A happy person is normally a successful person. Once we find true meaning in life, then happiness is merely a by-product of that; not only happiness and joy, but success, satisfaction and most of all, our purpose for living.

Let us follow the Word of God that says, "Seek first the kingdom of God and His righteousness, and all these things shall be added to you" (Matt. 6:33). Pursue Jesus and joy and happiness will follow.

Passing on Your Legacy

He will turn the hearts of the fathers to the children, and the hearts of the children to their fathers.

~ Malachi 4:6

As fathers we cannot change the weather, the value of our currency, or the cost of living. But there is one thing we can do and that is to hand over our legacy to the next generation.

Handing over a farm to a son is a very sensitive matter. The first thing we need to understand is that farming is not a business; it is a way of life. We live our job.

Normally when a father hands his farm over to his son, he keeps living there, observing his son's every decision and action. This can be awkward for both of them, because the son will probably not farm in the same way as his father did. In fact, the son might be more successful than his father ever was, or the other way around.

An adjustment needs to happen and the only way to do that is by talking to one another, extending grace and exercising much patience. The best way to do this is to hand over the farm completely. Some fathers are reluctant, saying, "But he could lose the farm!" That's true, but rather lose the farm and gain your son than lose both the farm *and* your son. This principle is true for handing over any business to your children.

Use It or Lose It

"Because you are lukewarm, and neither cold nor hot, I will vomit you out of My mouth."

~ Revelation 3:16

In rugby there is the adage "use it or lose it." You must get involved; you cannot hang around the edges. We need to get more proactive in our families, in our country and in our place of work. We need to be producing goodness and positivity; we need to build up the nation. We need to keep on keeping on for Jesus.

I firmly believe that the best is yet to come for those who are positive in their outlook and who trust in the Lord Jesus Christ in every circumstance.

Think of the parable of the talents and how one of the servants simply buried the talent his master had given him (see Matt. 25:14-30). When the master returned, he was angry that the man had not put it to good use by investing it. The master took the talent away from him and gave it to the servant who had increased his money.

God blesses those who use what He gives them. Those who are too fearful to go ahead in faith will lose even that which they already have.

Seek Godly Counsel

The king answered them roughly. King Rehoboam rejected the advice of the elders.

~ 2 Chronicles 10:13

We need godly counsel like never before. We have a situation where people are desperately trying to make ends meet; we are facing corruption on every side, our currency is losing ground and the prevailing drought is threatening our livelihood.

In 2 Chronicles 10 we read the story of a young king who took over from his father. At first, the young king sought counsel from his father's advisors. They said, "If you are kind to these people, and please them, and speak good words to them, they will be your servants forever" (2 Chron. 10:7). Unfortunately, he rejected their counsel and instead consulted the young men who had grown up with him.

When the king asked the young men for advice, they told him to make the load heavier. The king spoke to his people in an unkind manner, with no grace, no gentleness and no godly wisdom. He threatened the people and the results were disastrous.

People are much more important than statistics. Without wise people in this beloved country of ours, we cannot be successful in the long run. God wants us to do things His way and seek godly wisdom from those wiser than us.

Complete the Mission

David said to Solomon: "My son, as for me, it was in my mind to build a house to the name of the LORD my God; but the word of the LORD came to me, saying, 'You have shed much blood and have made great wars; you shall not build a house for My name. Behold, a son shall be born to you, who shall be a man of rest … He shall build a house for My name.'"

~ 1 Chronicles 22:7-10

God has given each of us a responsibility and we should not allow the cares of this world to hamstring us. We need to continue with the operation God has given us.

We need to stand on the promises of God; if we do that, we will ultimately succeed. Sometimes it is a very daunting task to step into the shoes of our parents or those who have gone before us, but by the grace of God we can do it – just like Solomon did what God told him to do through his father, David.

So let us strive to complete the task we have been given by God. If we do so, God will see to it that we are able to complete the vision He has called us to fulfil.

Simple Obedience

"It is easier for heaven and earth to pass away than for one tittle of the law to fail."

~ Luke 16:17

God's Word never fails. The Bible remains steadfast; it never changes and is always perfectly relevant in all situations.

In the verse for today, Jesus says that nothing in the Word of God will ever fail. Whatever God has said in the Bible *will* happen. There are conditions in the Word of God, however, in both the Old and New Testaments. I want to qualify right at the outset that no one knows grace more than people like myself.

I am a sinner saved by grace. I am fully aware of it, but I cannot, once I have heard the truth of God through the Word, hide behind it. If I make a mistake, I need to confess it and then move on. I cannot sin purposefully, knowing it is wrong, and disregard the consequences. Jesus says, "You will know them by their fruits. Do men gather grapes from thornbushes or figs from thistles?" (Matt. 7:16).

We need to take the Word of God as it is written and live accordingly, then we will be deemed holy men and women of the Lord. The meaning of the word *holiness* is ultimately a person who is simply obedient.

The Value of Wisdom

If you receive my words, and treasure my commands within you, so that you incline your ear to wisdom, and apply your heart to understanding; yes, if you cry out for discernment … then you will understand the fear of the LORD, and find the knowledge of God.

~ Proverbs 2:1-3, 5

We once had an old gentlemen in our district who had a better knowledge of cattle than anyone I've ever met. In fact, when he farmed in Kenya as a young man, before he had relocated to South Africa, he won the farmer of the year award.

He would have loved to have met with the young farmers and taught them all the things he had learned in his life. But the young men didn't seem to have time to listen to him … always too busy. I suppose we are all guilty of that, but we must remember that sometimes a shortcut is not the quickest or best way home.

Of course, we know that the greatest Advisor is the Holy Spirit. If we look at John 16:7, Jesus clearly says that He is leaving so that He can send us a Helper, who is the Holy Spirit.

Let us consult Him first and foremost, because He is available and wants to help us gain true wisdom.

Genuine Contentment

Now godliness with contentment is great gain.

~ 1 Timothy 6:6

Benjamin Franklin once said, "Content makes poor men rich; discontent makes rich men poor." Maybe you and I need to ask ourselves a very serious question today and that is: How much is enough?

I remember arriving in South Africa from Zambia over 40 years ago; my greatest desire was to have my own farm once again. After a lot of blood, sweat and tears, that dream was realised, but I was still not content.

Contentment only came after I had met the Lord Jesus Christ, who filled me with His peace. In John 14:27, Jesus reminds us: "Peace I leave with you, My peace I give to you. Let not your heart be troubled, neither let it be afraid."

Let us start concentrating on what we can do for others, rather than always trying to satisfy our own needs. There is such joy in giving freely to someone in need. It is in giving that we receive, so the Lord tells us: "Freely you have received, freely give" (Matt. 10:8).

When we understand what God has done for us, then it is easy for us not only to be *generous* with what we have, but also *content* with what we have.

Women of Valour

An excellent wife is the crown of her husband, but she who causes shame is like rottenness in his bones.

~ Proverbs 12:4

It feels like only yesterday that Jill and I along with our five children drove all the way from the central province of Zambia via Swaziland to KwaZulu-Natal, arriving on a farm that was literally a piece of neglected ground. At the time, it was all we could afford to buy.

We hired a small caravan for three weeks and then proceeded to unpack. We cut down the trees, pulled out the roots, ploughed the land and started to cultivate a crop of seed maize.

There were no dams or boreholes on the property and for the first few days my poor wife had to take buckets and drive 5 km to get water for drinking and to wash the children, until a neighbour very kindly lent us his water cart.

We had a bumper crop of maize that year and that was the start of our farming enterprise. This did not happen because I was a good farmer. No, it happened because I have an excellent wife.

We thank God for the womenfolk in our lives. They are the backbone of society. Without them, us men would be somewhat lost. Let us never forget to cherish our wives, sisters and mothers.

Respect for God and Others

Respect everyone, and love the family of believers. Fear God.

~ 1 Peter 2:17 NLT

We need to respect God. He is not to be referred to as the "boss," the "man upstairs" or "my mate." He is the Creator of Heaven and earth, and He is not to be taken advantage of.

We also need to respect each other, whether we are working with colleagues, employees or employers – we need to respect them as God's creation and as fellow people. We must respect one another and we must not antagonize each other.

Remember, the greatest commandment in the Bible is found in Mark 12:29-31, "The first of all the commandments is: 'Hear, O Israel, the LORD our God, the LORD is one. And you shall love the LORD your God with all your heart, with all your soul, with all your mind, and with all your strength.' This is the first commandment. And the second, like it, is this: 'You shall love your neighbor as yourself.' There is no other commandment greater than these."

We need to show respect for all people, whether at work, at home or at the sports club; and we need to show respect to God, our Father and Lord of all.

Guard against Negative Talk

Keep your heart with all diligence, for out of it spring the issues of life.

~ Proverbs 4:23

We should do our best to avoid negative and sinful talk, which can so easily contaminate the wellspring of our hearts. Job, a farmer, made a covenant not to speak evil words or to listen to negative people. We, too, need to guard against negative things penetrating the spring of living water in our hearts. In other words, we must not muddy the purity of our hearts by the evil things of this world.

"If you have nothing good to say, don't say anything at all," is what our parents teach us when we are young. We should rather encourage and affirm those around us. We need to be very careful and watch what is in our hearts; be mindful of what we say and choose carefully what we read and watch on TV and social media. Doing so can help us develop a positive outlook on life and even change the trajectory of our lives.

Robert Orben, a comedy writer, once remarked that "a compliment is verbal sunshine." Try to avoid the cynics, the complainers and those who speak negatively. Negativity is profoundly harmful, especially for dynamic, optimistic people. Let us rather speak life over our beloved country.

Attempt Less, Achieve More

"Seek first the kingdom of God and His righteousness, and all these things shall be added to you."

~ Matthew 6:33

*P*riority is a very important word in the Christian's daily life and Jesus reminds us of this in the Scripture for today. Charles Spurgeon once wrote, "In the long run, we shall do more by sometimes doing less." Wise words indeed!

There is no future for a lazy man because his business will eventually collapse, but we need to be equally careful about becoming workaholics. Instead, we need to specialise in a certain area. In this way we will be able to achieve more by doing less. Quantity is not always the answer. In the cut-throat business of agriculture, for instance, it seems that quality currently plays a far more important role than quantity.

We need to look after ourselves, our families, our staff and our colleagues before it is too late. By putting priorities in place we will achieve a lot more than by running around aimlessly and attempting to do too much. Let us aim for balance and always be mindful of bringing glory to God in all that we do.

Obedience to God

Even after we had suffered before and were spitefully treated at Philippi, as you know, we were bold in our God to speak to you the gospel of God in much conflict.

~ 1 Thessalonians 2:2

Our conduct and the way in which we behave is extremely important. In today's verse, we read that Paul's conduct was not influenced by trying to please others, rather by being totally obedient to God.

We each need to run our own race. Amongst other things, this means avoiding the temptation to keep up with the Joneses. Just because your neighbour has bought a brand-new vehicle does not mean that you must go and do the same. Our conduct must reflect the confidence that we have in Christ Jesus and trying to find favour with Him, rather than trying to find favour with others. Don't seek people's approval; our reward comes from God alone.

We should not seek glory or recognition from man, because people are fickle: Today you are a hero, tomorrow the world wants to chase you away. Our reward comes from the Lord Jesus Christ Himself. We need to be kinder and gentler.

Our labour and effort is for an eternal reward, not for temporal things.

Setting the Right Example

"Let your light so shine before men, that they may see your good works and glorify your Father in heaven."

~ Matthew 5:16

The single biggest need in our country, and indeed the world, might well be the need for godly fathers. We need more fathers to be good examples to their children and to lead from the front, so that young men and women know how they should live.

We need fathers and mentors who are godly examples and who retain godly principles in the home and in the workplace. As sons, we need to make a determined effort to appreciate our fathers and to reassure them of our support and love, because they are subject to pressures many of us don't understand.

As fathers we need to thank God for the wonderful privilege we have of being called "Dad." It is a joy and a blessing to see one's children grow up in a righteous and God-fearing manner.

We must not dominate our families and try to rule the home with an iron fist, but rather be the leader, protector and loving force in our homes for our children, and when the time comes, for our grandchildren. Let us set the right example wherever we go.

A Personal Choice

He will judge everyone according to what they have done. He will give eternal life to those who keep on doing good, seeking after the glory and honor and immortality that God offers.

~ Romans 2:6-7 NLT

In the Kingdom, there are no "grandchildren" – there are only children of God. If you are a believer, it is not a guarantee that your child or your grandchild will be admitted into Heaven on the strength of your commitment to Jesus.

Each person has got to meet Jesus Christ in their own personal way. By the same token, no child is liable for the salvation of their parents. Of course, we pray desperately for our loved ones, but we cannot be held accountable if they refuse to bow the knee and follow Jesus Christ.

Each one of us has got to meet with Jesus Christ ourselves. We can direct others down the right road, but we cannot compel them to be converted. Only the Holy Spirit can do that and only the desire in the individual's heart can make it happen. They say you can lead a horse to water, but you can't make him drink. That is very true of salvation.

Let each one of us make sure that we are good examples to those in the world and then pray that our loved ones might find their way to Jesus.

Now Is the Time

"Do you not say, 'There are still four months and then comes the harvest'? Behold, I say to you, lift up your eyes and look at the fields, for they are already white for harvest!"

~ John 4:35

In Luke 16:19-31, Jesus tells the story of a rich man who was clothed in fine apparel and dined sumptuously every day. Then we meet a poor man, a beggar named Lazarus who had nothing, but loved Jesus.

When Lazarus died, he went straight to Heaven; when the rich man died, he went to hell. The rich man cried out to Abraham and asked if Lazarus could bring him some water. But Abraham said that the chasm between Heaven and hell was too big.

Then the man asked if Abraham could send Lazarus back to earth to warn his brothers of hell. But Abraham said that if they did not pay attention to Moses and the prophets, neither would they be persuaded to listen to someone who had risen from the dead.

The Lord is saying that now is the hour of salvation; not once you die, but now. This is the time to tell people about Jesus Christ. We need to pray that our loved ones will accept Jesus Christ as their Lord and Saviour. There is no other way to Heaven and there is no other way by which a person can be saved.

Until the Harvest …

"The kingdom of heaven is like a man who sowed good seed in his field … At the time of harvest I will say to the reapers, 'First gather together the tares and bind them in bundles to burn them, but gather the wheat into my barn.'"
~ Matthew 13:24, 30

God did not take sin out of the world; instead, He sent His Son, Jesus Christ, to earth. Many of us are so concerned about the evil and the sin in this world that we forget the solution: Jesus Christ.

Remember the parable of the sower: a farmer sowed good seed but the devil came at night and sowed tares (weeds) into the same field. We need to concentrate on Jesus and not on the evil (the weeds) of this world. Stop concentrating on the evil, corruption and immorality of the world. Instead, we should focus on the power and goodness of Jesus Christ and fix our eyes on Him alone. When we do that, we will clearly distinguish the evil of this world and we will be wise and successful.

Separate yourself from the gossip mongers and the negative agents of this world. Until Jesus returns, let us spend time with those who have the same heart as us: worshipping and loving Jesus Christ with all we have.

Show Kindness

"Whoever gives one of these little ones only a cup of cold water in the name of a disciple, assuredly, I say to you, he shall by no means lose his reward."

~ Matthew 10:42

While reading the Word of God one morning, I read the account of kindness shown by King David towards the cripple Mephibosheth in 2 Samuel 9:1-13.

He was the son of David's best friend, Jonathan, who died fighting the enemy with his father, King Saul. When David found out about Jonathan's only surviving son, he brought the young man out of poverty and into his palace, and gave him a place at the royal table to eat with the king every day.

He also restored to Mephibosheth all of his grandfather's land and possessions, simply because of David's friendship and love for Jonathan.

If you and I really love Jesus, then we too should honour Him by loving and caring for all of His children. Especially the very least of them because the Word of God says in Matthew 25:40, "Inasmuch as you did it to one of the least of these My brethren, you did it to Me."

Be kind and considerate to your colleagues, your friends and to strangers. Respect your elders, remembering that you too will one day get old. Do all you can to sow good into the Kingdom of God.

June

He gives us grace and glory. The Lord will withhold no good thing from those who do what is right.

~ *Psalm 84:11* NLT ~

When in Doubt

Jesus said, "Blessed are those who have not seen and yet have believed."

~ John 20:29

Horatius Bonar said, "All unbelief is the belief of a lie." Truly, it must be the one sin that we all commit which really hurts our Lord Jesus! Doubt is what holds people back from believing God. Doubt is the very thing that will keep you from a miracle. We need faith to believe the truth.

We so often readily believe the lies of this world and then question God's written Word. Even if it is only subconsciously that we say, "I do not believe it," it must cause tremendous pain to our Lord and Saviour.

During Pentecost, Jesus told His disciples that it was beneficial for them (and for all of us), that He go to His Father so that He could send us the Helper, His Holy Spirit.

Allow the Holy Spirit to fill you with His promises, His love and His hope for the future. Romans 8:11 says that it is the same Holy Spirit that raised Christ from the dead who desires to work a miracle in our lives.

Let us not restrict His workings through our unbelief.

Trust the Helper

"I will pray the Father, and He will give you another Helper, that He may abide with you forever."

~ John 14:16

Jesus told us very clearly in John 16:7 that it was to our advantage that He went away. For if He did not go, the Helper would not have come to us. Rather that He depart and send the Holy Spirit to us.

The Holy Spirit is the One who is known as the Comforter, Counsellor and Helper. He is also known as the Advocate, Teacher, Seal on God's people and Guide.

Stop trying to do things in your own strength and allow the Holy Spirit, who is our Comforter, Encourager, Counsellor and Advocate to take control of your situation today.

They always say that a farmer makes a plan. Well, I can honestly say that not one of my plans have ever worked when I tried to go it alone. The ploy of the devil is to make us proud and then get us to do things our way. We usually fail miserably.

Trust the Helper today and allow Him to direct your ways in conjunction with God's Word. You will be regarded as wise because of the quality of the decisions you make.

Judge Not

"Judge not, that you be not judged. For with what judgment you judge, you will be judged; and with the measure you use, it will be measured back to you."

~ Matthew 7:1-2

The Lord Jesus warns us to be careful that we do not judge others, for we shall be judged by the exact same measure that we use to judge others.

How often do we pass judgement on someone who is down and out, yet we do not know the reason why they find themselves in that particular predicament? Because a man, for example, is poor or unemployed, it doesn't give us any reason to think that he is not smart. We need to exert mercy just like Jesus did and try to build the person up to believe in himself again.

If you feel you cannot help someone who is down-hearted, start to seriously pray for them to find a job rather than to judge them as being lazy or incompetent.

Remember, it is only by the grace of God that we are not in that person's shoes, so let us concentrate on building them up rather than judging them.

Sound the Alarm

But if the watchman sees the enemy coming and doesn't sound the alarm to warn the people, he is responsible for their captivity. They will die in their sins, but I will hold the watchman responsible for their deaths.

~ Ezekiel 33:6 NLT

It is time to blow the trumpet and to sound the alarm. I believe the rampant sin we see today is because people have no more fear of God. The church is asleep and "the watchman" is not warning the people to turn from their iniquity and respect God and Creation.

The enemy is on the prowl and inciting people to do what they please. Violence, lawlessness, immorality and blatant corruption abound and everyone keeps quiet about it. The Church, which means you and I, are the conscience of the nation! The unbeliever does not know any better.

We need to become more vocal, to call sin by its name and to stand up for the outcasts, the innocent, the young and the vulnerable, and to tell society that Jesus Christ is a holy and righteous God who will not tolerate sin.

We need to sound the alarm today. When a nation turns back to God wholeheartedly, then revival will come and that alone will put an end to the prevailing chaos in the world today.

Look Up!

Seek the LORD and His strength; seek His face evermore!

~ 1 Chronicles 16:11

It is said that a rut in the road is just like a shallow grave. You need to get out of it as soon as you can otherwise you will perish.

I was jogging early one morning. I had my head down and was concentrating on where I was running. As the first rays of sunshine started to break through, I felt the Holy Spirit tell me to lift up my head. I looked up and saw a beautiful crystal clear sky with a pink tinge as the sun was coming out.

I also saw a plane flying very high up in the sky and behind it a long distinct vapour which was a bright red colour. It looked like a sharp arrow, and the Lord reminded me again to lift up my head, to keep out of the rut, and to focus and complete the work that He has called me to!

Luke 21:28 says, "Look up and lift up your heads, because your redemption draws near." Get out of that rut and look to the Lord, because the Second Coming is nearer than we think.

A Powerful Word from Scripture

"For God so loved the world that He gave His only begotten Son, that whoever believes in Him should not perish but have everlasting life."

~ John 3:16

The whole Bible can be summed up by this Scripture verse:

For God so loved the world ... Love is indeed the most powerful single force in the universe.

That He gave His only begotten Son ... only by the grace of God would I be able to offer up one of my sons for a sinful man. For in my own strength I definitely would not be able to do it.

That whoever believes in Him ... Without faith it is impossible to be a follower of Christ Jesus. Remember, faith is to believe what you cannot see, but the reward of that faith is to see what you believe.

Should not perish ... Remember that the spirit of a man never perishes. But the more important question is where will you spend eternity?

But have everlasting life ... If we believe, we will spend eternity with Jesus in Heaven.

Meditate today on what Christ did for you on Calvary!

Feelings of Loneliness

"Fear not, for I am with you; be not dismayed, for I am your God. I will strengthen you, yes, I will help you, I will uphold you with My righteous right hand."

~ Isaiah 41:10

If you are feeling lonely today, there is one person who can truly identify with you and that is our beloved Saviour, Jesus Christ.

Take a moment to think about the enormity of what Christ did for all mankind. Will we ever be able to fully grasp what He had to endure on the Cross?

Jesus said to His disciples in Matthew 26:40 when He asked them to watch and wait with Him, "What! Could you not watch with Me one hour?" The disciples had fallen asleep, leaving the Master to pray alone.

I looked up the meaning of the word *loneliness* and it means solitary, remote or sad because one has no friends or company.

So if you are feeling that way today, there is One who knows how you feel. Speak to Him because He says He will never leave you nor forsake you (see Heb. 13:5).

A Selfish Heart

Let nothing be done through selfish ambition or conceit, but in lowliness of mind let each esteem others better than himself.

~ Philippians 2:3

Our biggest enemy in life is not only the devil. His neck was broken on the Cross of Calvary! Our arch-enemy number one is "self": me, myself and I. Self-centredness is a killer.

Jesus said in Matthew 11:11 that there has never risen one greater than John the Baptist. Why we may ask, seeing that there are so many other giants of the faith in the Bible.

I believe it is quite simply because he was completely focused on the Lord and had no concern for himself. This man, the most popular evangelist of his time, who was drawing in multitudes, said that he was not even worthy to carry Jesus' shoes.

Let us ask God today to help deliver us from ourselves and we will truly start to experience liberty, freedom and happiness and in turn be free to help others.

Standing Strong

He will not be afraid of evil tidings; His heart is steadfast, trusting in the LORD.

~ Psalm 112:7

If we look at Judges 8:20-21, we will see that Gideon's son Jether was afraid because he was still young and would not draw his sword to kill the enemy. So his father, Gideon, who was called the Mighty Man of Valour by the angel of the Lord, drew his sword and killed the enemy without hesitation.

When you know who you are in Christ, you will have the strength to finish the race. Daniel 11:32 says that the people who know their God shall be strong and carry out great exploits.

In this life we do not always have it easy. There are so many things that cause grief, sorrow and pain. The good news is that we can take our tears and our sorrow to the Lord. He will comfort us and heal us. He will give us His strength.

Let us spend more time with God today and less time trying to make our own plans. The difference it will make to your life will soon be visible. You have to spend time with Him so that He can give you His joy which is your strength.

Watch the Hills

I will lift up my eyes to the hills – from whence comes my help? My help comes from the LORD, who made heaven and earth.

~ Psalm 121:1-2

I find such peace and inner strength just by gazing at the hills … to think that they have stood there from the very beginning of time and will still be there when we are no longer on this earth. Yet with all the beauty, majesty and strength that the hills display, our hope is not found there. No, our hope lies completely in the saving, protecting and undeserved grace of Jesus.

The psalmist continues in verse 3 and says that God alone will ensure that not even our foot will slip. In fact, He will watch over you and me day and night, as God does not sleep! He is our Protector.

The Master has promised us that as long as we keep our eyes fixed on Him, He will help us finish this race. He shall preserve us from all evil.

Enjoy His creation, the hills and the mountaintops, for they are truly magnificent because they give us a glimpse of the incredibly artistic and creative God we serve. Never forget that our help comes from Jesus Christ alone.

Jesus Christ Is the Word

In the beginning was the Word, and the Word was with God, and the Word was God.

~ John 1:1

Jesus Christ is the Word. If someone asks you to show them Jesus, then give them a Bible.

I always tell people that I am not interested in their opinions and that they should not be interested in my opinion either. All we are to be concerned about is God's opinion on the matter.

We need to use God's Holy Word as our guide in this turbulent life or else we shall lose our way completely.

I read a very troubling statement from a prominent pastor in the USA who said that the church will become even more irrelevant if it continues to quote letters from 2 000 years ago as their best defence. We are truly in the last days. Be very careful who you listen to. If a message does not line up with God's Holy Word then disregard it completely.

Like never before we need to meditate on the Word and bury it in our hearts in order not to become deceived and misled by the system of this world. Psalm 119:105 says, "Your word is a lamp to my feet and a light to my path." Make sure you stay in the light.

Freedom in Christ

So when Jesus had received the sour wine, He said, "It is finished!" And bowing His head, He gave up His spirit.

~ John 19:30

Your freedom in Christ came at a cost; a very expensive one at that. So don't exchange it for anything or anyone. Jesus paid for our freedom on the cross of Calvary when He said, "It is finished." Be careful not to trade it for temporary worldly things.

When we dabble in sin, telling that white lie, continuing with the immoral relationship, bending the rules ever so slightly, or even stealing, then we forfeit our freedom. How? Well, once the devil gets a foot in the door, he does not stop there. For example, that so-called innocent relationship with that married person usually leads to more and eventually ends in adultery.

That little lie often has to be followed up with a bigger lie and eventually the lies catch up with you. When you start breaking the rules, it is difficult to stop. It becomes a vicious cycle.

Jesus said, "If the Son makes you free, you shall be free indeed" (John 8:36). There is nothing on this earth that is worth giving up your God-given freedom for. Deal with your sin. Ask Jesus to give you the courage to confront it and move on in His godly freedom.

The Prayer of Faith

"Your faith has made you well. Go in peace."

~ Luke 8:48

God does not answer prayer, He answers the prayer of faith … there is a big difference.

Some time ago we prepared for a huge miracle to take place on the coast of KwaZulu-Natal. We believed that the Rain Maker, Jesus Christ, would hear our prayers.

First of all we prayed prayers of repentance. Secondly, we prayed for sustaining rain. We prayed for the towns already under water restrictions and for the farmers who were losing their precious crops due to the severe drought.

Jesus said to the centurion that He had not found such great faith in all of Israel! The centurion told Jesus that He just had to speak the word and his servant would be healed. And it happened (see Matt. 8:5-13).

You see, it is in believing that we receive (see Matt. 21:22). It's all about believing – believing that Jesus Christ is the Son of God, believing that He is a miracle worker and believing that He is the same yesterday, today and forever (see Heb. 13:8). Having faith in God puts Him in the right place: at the forefront of our lives.

Like Father, Like Son

Imitate me, just as I also imitate Christ.

~ 1 Corinthians 11:1

Our children hardly ever do what we tell them to do. They do what they see us do. In Ephesians 5:1-2 we read that we are to be followers of God. It basically means that we have to imitate Jesus in all that we do.

The Lord showed me clearly in my quiet time one morning that the difference between a servant and a son or daughter is genes. If we are children of God, then we have His genes. His nature, personality and characteristics are the fruit of the Spirit that flow through our lives if we follow in Jesus' steps (see Gal. 5:22-23).

Try today to spend more time with your Heavenly Father, then try it every day for a week and let it become a habit in your life. You will see how you become more like Him as you spend time in His presence!

Always ask yourself before you act or say something, "Does this look like my Father?" For example: "I love others because He loves. I forgive because He forgives. I give because He gives."

Let us display those heavenly genes as we go about our daily walk.

Wisdom for the Way

So teach us to number our days, that we may gain a heart of wisdom.

~ Psalm 90:12

While seeking after God for a special word one day, I felt very strongly in my spirit that He was saying to me, "Wait on the LORD" (Ps. 27:14). I knew that God would show me what to do, what to say and where to go.

The Lord does not want us to make rash decisions. When we make hasty plans, we allow ourselves to be pressured into making decisions that could later cost us dearly.

Instead, the Father wants us to be mature and to pray earnestly before committing to anything. When you've spent time with the Lord and you truly feel that He has told you to go a certain route in your life or in business, set your face toward that goal and go for it with all you have.

When you take a step of faith, you can trust God to honour it. Remember that you don't have to be lonely during your times of decision-making because He is just one prayer away.

God bless you richly as you walk with Jesus through the exciting things He has planned for you.

The Ministry of Reconciliation

Now all things are of God, who has reconciled us to Himself through Jesus Christ, and has given us the ministry of reconciliation.

~ 2 Corinthians 5:18

The word *reconciliation* means to restore friendly relations. What a great opportunity to be an ambassador of Christ. This is exactly what our Father has called us to be, His ambassadors, bringing reconciliation between God and people!

I'm so grateful that I know Jesus Christ as my Lord and Saviour. If it weren't for Him, I don't know where I'd be today or, more to the point, where my family would be. Because I've met Him and because He showed me my faults, I have been able to rectify many of them. I can now speak honestly to my children. They know I'm not perfect – far from it – but they also know that God is not finished with me yet.

Spend lots of time with your loved ones. Ask for forgiveness, even if it's not entirely your fault. Respect one another and God will heal those wounds and those misunderstandings.

Let every day be a God-given opportunity to build bridges, love unconditionally and be the reconcilers Jesus has called us to be.

Folly of the Godless

The crown of the wise is their riches, but the foolishness of fools is folly.

~ Proverbs 14:24

Folly means foolishness. To say that there is no God is extreme folly! As King David said in Psalm 53:1, "The fool has said in his heart, 'There is no God.'"

God is everywhere. As I'm writing this in my quiet time room on the farm, I hear the birds singing outside my window. I know that our God created this beautiful music. Even His creation is singing praises to Him. Just about every single Bible prophecy has come to pass, and Jesus' Second Coming is very evident.

Let us not waste valuable time trying to refute the existence of God, let us rather increase our faith by believing the Bible. Tell the world about the imminent return of Jesus who so loved us that He died on a cross for our sins. He made a way for each one of us to walk this road of life with peace, purpose and victory.

Remember, Jesus is not coming back for good people; He's coming back for believers. He is coming back for those who know God. Because of that single act of faith, the believer shall carry out great exploits for God in these last days.

Keep Going

I pray that from His glorious, unlimited resources He will empower you with inner strength through His Spirit.

~ Ephesians 3:16 NLT

We're halfway through the year and I'm sure many of us might have experienced a few disappointments so far. Maybe you did not quite succeed in your goals thus far.

Well, you are not alone because the apostle Paul, who wrote two-thirds of the New Testament, and who had a personal, one-on-one encounter with the living Christ said, "Not that I have already attained, or am already perfected; but I press on, that I may lay hold of that for which Christ Jesus has also laid hold of me" (Phil. 3:12).

Sometimes we say, "Lord, this is too difficult. I can't go through this fiery trial." Then He says, "You can. Just keep going. Out of My glorious riches I will fill you with power through My Spirit."

We need to keep going and not lose heart because He who calls us is faithful (see 1 Thess. 5:24).

I honestly believe with all my heart that the best is yet to come for those who believe. God bless you as you take that leap of faith!

Counting the Cost

He said to another, "Follow Me." But he said, "Lord, let me first go and bury my father." Jesus said to him, "Let the dead bury their own dead, but you go and preach the kingdom of God."

~ Luke 9:59-60

I'm reminded often by the Lord during my quiet time that we need to really sit down and count the cost of being a follower of Jesus as His Second Coming is drawing closer. Basically, if our faith and allegiance to Jesus Christ in these last days is costing us nothing, then it is actually worth nothing.

In Luke 9:57-62, we read of many people wanting to follow after Jesus, but every single time discipleship came at a cost and sacrifices were required. We have to take up our own cross if we want to follow Jesus.

How much time do you spend alone with God at the moment? Do you have quiet times in His presence at all? If you want to be a follower of Jesus you cannot afford not to spend time with Him. Jesus is the One who will give you the strength for everyday life. Count the cost of following the Lord wholeheartedly today.

Joy Comes in the Morning

The faithful love of the Lord never ends! His mercies never cease. Great is His faithfulness; His mercies begin afresh each morning.

~ Lamentations 3:22-23 NLT

I remember when the Lord clearly spoke to me through Psalm 30. It felt like I had been in the proverbial pit with no light at the end of the tunnel for a long time. But one morning the weeping was over and joy filled my heart to overflowing. God assured me that He was going to perform something extraordinary at one of the events I was hosting!

Whenever I feel downcast, I'm reminded over and over that the Lord is my Helper and He will turn my mourning into dancing (see Ps. 30:11).

We need to stand up and be counted today. We are fighting a war. But the good news is that we've got all the weapons in Heaven and earth at our disposal. We have the power of Christ in us. And by His power we should tell all people around us that Jesus loves them.

We should tell them that when they accept Jesus Christ as their Lord and Saviour they also will be more than conquerors through Him who loves us. We should tell them there is hope, there is a better way and there is a future. His name is Jesus Christ.

Who Will You Serve?

Choose for yourselves this day whom you will serve ... But as for me and my house, we will serve the LORD.

~ Joshua 24:15

We need to decide whom we will serve. Believers are required to make serious decisions and commit themselves fully to being followers of Jesus Christ.

Jesus made it very clear that if we are not for Him, then we are against Him (see Matt. 12:30).

I firmly believe God has chosen you and me for a time such as this and that we have a vital role to play in the destiny of this confused, depraved and desperate world we are living in.

The sovereignty and authenticity of God's Word is at stake these days. Folk have no fear or regard for God's written instructions any longer. But when we mess with the written Word of God, we mess with Jesus!

As believers we are called to make it clear that we serve God. We are also called to tell others about Jesus and that the time to believe in Him and serve Him is now.

Never Forget God

"And you shall remember the LORD your God, for it is He who gives you power to get wealth, that He may establish His covenant which He swore to your fathers, as it is this day."

~ Deuteronomy 8:18

Time is running out. How much worse must things get before we call upon our Father to intervene on our behalf?

This is not the responsibility of the unbeliever; it is the obligation and command of each believer in this nation right now!

The Word of God states very clearly in 2 Chronicles 7:14, "If My people who are called by My name will humble themselves, and pray and seek My face, and turn from their wicked ways, then I will hear from heaven, and will forgive their sin and heal their land."

We need to stand together. You see, when you are persistent with God, He will always respond to you. If you let others shush you or take away your resolve, you'll get nowhere.

Conversely, if you are resolute and remain determined in asking God to intervene for you and for this nation you will see an answer. If ever we need God to intervene, it is now!

Call on His Name

For whosoever shall call upon the name of the Lord shall be saved.

~ Romans 10:13 KJV

The time is now for the "whosoevers" – meaning everyone and anyone – to enter into the Kingdom of God! People need the Lord desperately. They want answers. They want them straight and simple, just like the Master spoke when He walked on the earth.

The prodigal son needs to know that he is welcome back home whenever he wants to return. The prostitutes must know that their sins are forgiven, and that they must go and sin no more. The widow needs to know Jesus will be to her the husband she does not have. The orphan must know that he has a father in Heaven.

As followers of Christ, we need to step out into the world and tell the broken-hearted, the guilty, so-called failures, the confused and the fearful that Jesus loves them and wants to save them.

Jesus is the judge, and His Word says, "For whosoever shall call upon the name of the Lord shall be saved." (Rom. 10:13 KJV). Whosoever? Yes. Whosoever calls on the name of the Lord shall be saved. No matter when you called on His name, early or late in your life. You will be saved.

Lighten the Load

Let us lay aside every weight, and the sin which so easily ensnares us, and let us run with endurance the race that is set before us.

~ Hebrews 12:1

In the book of Acts, we read that when Paul's ship sailed to Rome and into a severe storm, they got rid of all their excess weight. They threw overboard all their tackle and merchandise in order for the ship to be saved. As it turned out the ship was shipwrecked on the shores of Malta, but the good news was that not one passenger drowned.

Sometimes we also need to get rid of the excess baggage in our lives that we are dragging along.

As I write to you the Lord Jesus is impressing on my heart that you are carrying around on your back a bag so heavy it feels like a bag of cement and it consists of all the things that weigh you down: unforgiveness, anger, fear, hatred, you name it.

It is making you tired and causing you to lose direction. You are losing hope and even becoming depressed as the storms of life increase. As a result you are starting to sink!

Jesus says very clearly to you today, "Give all your worries and cares to God, for He cares about you" (1 Pet. 5:7 NLT).

Just Do It!

"For I know the thoughts that I think toward you," says the LORD, "thoughts of peace and not of evil, to give you a future and a hope."

~ Jeremiah 29:11

Once you have been commissioned by God for a specific task in His Kingdom, then get on with it: "Just do it." Stop talking about it, and start doing it.

A young man approached me one Sunday morning and asked me if I would pray for him. He said that I had prayed for him when he was sixteen years old. He was now over forty years old. We had been praying for people to get actively involved in serving Jesus.

Sadly, he told me, with tears running down his face, that he had done nothing about it for all those years. The man basically asked if it was too late to start over again. With great joy I told him that it is never too late.

Never forget that the road to hell is paved with good intentions, so no more procrastination. As God's children, let us finish what we have started in our journey of faith.

Galatians 6:9 says, "And let us not grow weary while doing good, for in due season we shall reap if we do not lose heart."

Jesus Never Overlooks Anyone

"Assuredly, I say to you, inasmuch as you did it to one of the least of these My brethren, you did it to Me."

~ Matthew 25:40

In Numbers 2:31, we read that the tribe of Dan had to travel last, bringing up the rear of the twelve tribes of Israel.

From the outside looking in, one could think that they were possibly the most inferior of the tribes, but that assumption could not be further from the truth. You see, as the last tribe they had the enormous responsibility of collecting all the stragglers. All the disillusioned folk, the tired and sick folk, who have to be encouraged by the last tribe to keep on going.

We are all in for some huge surprises when we get to Heaven one day. I think the saints who will be heralded by God will be the old praying grannies, the mothers looking after God's children, the lonely missionaries, the Bible translators in the jungle, the school teachers who refuse to water down the Gospel and so many others who hardly get mentioned, or even noticed here on earth.

So press on, because your reward is awaiting you in Heaven. Jesus never overlooks anyone!

Speak Up!

Have no fellowship with the unfruitful works of darkness, but rather expose them.

~ Ephesians 5:11

Let us never cease to be motivated by the Holy Spirit to speak up when we see people sinning.

The apostle Paul could not contain himself; he had to warn the people, because God had given him such a love for those who were lost, directionless and literally grasping at straws! The philosophers called Paul a "babbler," meaning a seed picker, an idler who makes a living picking up scraps. How wrong they were.

I was called a "babbler" once too, but nevertheless, the truth always prevails, because God has put eternity into the heart of man. Eventually the most ardent critic will want to hear what you have to say, hence the invite to Paul from the philosophers to speak on Mars Hill, Athens.

If you work in an office, for instance, and you know that there are irregularities and possibly fraud, speak up – otherwise you will be a part of the problem. Instead of giving in to the crowd, stand up for God and the Lord will bless you.

Who knows what will happen when we speak up? Telling people about our faith cements our stand for Jesus Christ.

The Power of the Word

The word of God is living and powerful, and sharper than any two-edged sword, piercing even to the division of soul and spirit, and of joints and marrow, and is a discerner of the thoughts and intents of the heart.

~ Hebrews 4:12

As I was having my quiet time, I could hear the doves cooing outside. It was so very peaceful. Next to me a small fire glowed in the hearth. Jill had lovingly prepared it for me in order to take the chill off the early morning air.

I meditated on the goodness of God over the past number of years and the miraculous work He has done. I realised, yet again, the importance of preaching the undiluted Word of God (see 2 Tim. 4:2). Like never before there is a full onslaught on the authenticity of the Bible and yet people are just so hungry and desperate to learn more of the truth and power of God's Holy Word.

Jesus Himself is the Word, and He says, "I, if I am lifted up from the earth, will draw all peoples to Myself" (John 12:32). There is life and power in the Word of God.

The Time Is Now

"His preaching will turn the hearts of fathers to their children, and the hearts of children to their fathers. Otherwise I will come and strike the land with a curse."

~ Malachi 4:6 NLT

Father God tells us very clearly that it is the time for the hearts of the fathers to be turned towards the children and the hearts of the children to be turned towards their fathers.

There is no doubt in my mind that the Lord is putting this particular area of reconciliation very high on His priority list and He wants us to urgently cooperate with Him. It is the family unit that can make or break this nation, and the devil is working overtime to try and destroy this God-given gift of moms and dads, boys and girls.

The evil one knows just how precious to God the family unit is. He knows that if he can disrupt the family and bring division, divorce and rebellion into the family, he is on a winning streak.

Like never before, please pray for this fatherless generation that they may find the true meaning of life and for fathers to be reinstated to their rightful place as prophet, priest and king of their homes.

He Has Carried Me

He will feed His flock like a shepherd. He will carry the lambs in His arms, holding them close to His heart.

~ Isaiah 40:11 NLT

What grace, undeserved lovingkindness, unmerited favour, what love I have received from a most patient and loving God!

Reading in Isaiah 46:3-4 early one beautiful morning, God reminded me yet again how He has carried me through all these years. God says in His Word that from birth He upholds His children and He still carries me even to a grey old head.

He has promised to carry and deliver me! He shall do it for you, too, my dear friend, if you only put your trust in Jesus. It's the best insurance policy you could ever have.

Polycarp, bishop of Smyrna, was told by the Roman authorities to deny his faith in Christ and to swear by the divinity of Caesar. The saint's reply was, "Eighty-six years I have been His servant, and He has done me no wrong. How can I blaspheme my King who saved me?" And with that remark he died a martyr's death.

Fortunately, for all believers, we can confidently say with Paul the apostle, "For to me, to live is Christ, and to die is gain" (Phil. 1:21).

July

God is able to make all grace abound toward you,
that you, always having all sufficiency in all things,
may have an abundance for every good work.

~ 2 Corinthians 9:8 ~

Bear the Yoke

It is good for a man to bear the yoke in his youth.

~ Lamentations 3:27

A yoke is something you put over an ox when it is pulling a load. The writer of Lamentations says that when we are young, it is not a bad thing to feel the weight of a burden. We must not be afraid to bow our neck and take up our cross.

In Romans 5:3-4, Paul the apostle says, "We also glory in tribulations, knowing that tribulation produces perseverance; and perseverance, character; and character, hope." Hardship and perseverance develop the personality of a person.

I have never yet met a man worth his salt who has not been through fiery trials. Don't be afraid of burdens and to take up the yoke. It's in the suffering, in the times of hardship, that we learn and we build character.

For over 40 years I experienced many trials on our farm before the Lord released me to start preaching the Gospel full-time. Now, every time I see a person bow the knee and accept Jesus Christ as Lord and Saviour, it touches my heart deeply. I have walked the road of hard knocks well before God regarded me as fit and trustworthy to allow me to pray the Sinner's Prayer with His children.

Rooted in Christ

As you therefore have received Christ Jesus the Lord, so walk in Him, rooted and built up in Him and established in the faith, as you have been taught, abounding in it with thanksgiving.

~ Colossians 2:6-7

When people look at a ministry, they don't always know how it came to be established. For instance, ours has taken close to 40 years to grow. There is also an unseen part of a ministry: the inner life with God.

The "root" in the Christian life is faith. Romans 10:17 says, "So then faith comes by hearing, and hearing by the word of God." Our faith develops as we walk and live by faith.

At Shalom Ministries we are continually having communion with God, spending dedicated time with Him in the morning or evening in prayer and the Word of God. No one else can see this development of the roots.

If you want God to grow in your life and ministry and vision, be rooted deeply in the Lord and in His infallible Word. Remember what Jeremiah 17:7-8 (NLT) tells us: "Blessed are those who trust in the LORD and have made the LORD their hope and confidence. They are like trees planted along a riverbank, with roots that reach deep into the water. Such trees are not bothered by the heat or worried by long months of drought. They never stop producing fruit."

Proclaiming the Name of Jesus

Come with me, and see my zeal for the LORD.

~ 2 Kings 10:16

How enthusiastic are you about the Gospel of Jesus Christ? To what lengths will you go to proclaim the name of Jesus Christ, so that every knee will bow before Him and every tongue will confess that Jesus Christ is Lord (see Phil. 2:10)?

God opens doors for His children to proclaim the Good News. As life becomes more and more difficult, do not lose hope, for new opportunities will arise for us to testify about Him. People who didn't want to hear about the Bible or Jesus Christ a few years ago now ask, "What must I do to be saved?"

This is the time to be enthusiastic about Jesus and the precious Word of God. Remember, faith is a verb. And what does the Bible say about faith? It says, "Faith comes by hearing, and hearing by the word of God" (Rom. 10:17).

Pray in Line with God's Will

"Whatever you ask in My name, that I will do, that the Father may be glorified in the Son. If you ask anything in My name, I will do it. If you love Me, keep My commandments."
~ John 14:13-15

The secret to prayer is found in verse 15 of John 14 where the Lord says, "If you love Me, keep My commandments." If we ask in line with God's commandments, He will not fail us. This is quite simply because He cannot be untrue to His word.

The problem is that many of us ask amiss: We ask not according to the commandments of God, but according to our selfish desires.

I'm speaking purely from personal experience – I have said many times, "Lord, we need rain. If we don't get rain this crop will fail and then I will have no funds to continue the ministry of maintaining the church, of preaching the Gospel and of writing books." God has never failed me in over 40 years of growing crops on this farm.

Pray very carefully and seek the face of God. Seek His will for your life, for your family and for your vision; then humbly ask the Lord and He will answer your prayers.

The Importance of Inner Strength

He prayed that he might die, and said, "It is enough! Now, LORD, take my life, for I am no better than my fathers!"

~ 1 Kings 19:4

Elijah, a true man of God and one of my heroes, trusted God with extreme faith to bring down fire from Heaven, which consumed the sacrifice of the ox, the wood, the stones and the water in the trenches. He then proceeded to single-handedly kill 450 prophets of the devil. Because of one woman, Jezebel, who said that she would kill Elijah, he ran for his life, praying that he might die.

We need to be sure that as God blesses us outwardly, we strengthen ourselves inwardly. Otherwise, when we reach the goal, we will not be able to sustain it.

As you pray that God will use you in whatever area you have been called to, always be prepared to handle the success. If you don't, you'll get yourself into the same position as the prophet Elijah. He became tired and exhausted, and he allowed the lies of the devil to control his mind, sending him into a deep depression.

We need to come aside, give thanks to God and count our blessings one by one until the Lord uses us for the next exploit.

The Healing Hand of God

Let Israel now say – "If it had not been the LORD who was on our side, when men rose up against us, then they would have swallowed us alive, when their wrath was kindled against us."

~ Psalm 124:1-3

Where would we be if we had not given our lives to Jesus? Surely we would have been swallowed up. Often, I sit and meditate on how good the Lord has been to me throughout my life.

When I look back over the years, before I met Jesus Christ, there were so many times when He snatched me from the fowler's snare at the last moment and I didn't even know it.

In 2009, I was preaching my heart out to thousands of men. Then I suffered two heart attacks: one under the platform and a massive one at home. My blood pressure plummeted and I was literally dying. I remember lying spread out on the lawn in our garden with my family around me, but God intervened.

The emergency helicopter arrived to take me to the hospital. As the helicopter took off, I looked down and saw tens of thousands of hands reach up to the sky … men praying for me. If it had not been for God, I would have surely perished. Remember from whence you have come, lest you fall.

Walk the Talk

They profess to know God, but in works they deny Him, being abominable, disobedient, and disqualified for every good work.

~ Titus 1:16

Christians have to walk the talk. There are too many Christians who say they love God but by their actions they deny Him. An ethical and honest lifestyle is essential in order to win souls for Jesus.

In Luke 14:1, we read that the Pharisees were furious that Jesus had healed a man on the Sabbath. So Jesus asked them, "What man is there among you who has one sheep, and if it falls into a pit on the Sabbath, will not lay hold of it and lift it out?" (Matt. 12:11).

As a farmer, many times I have had to work on the Sabbath. We might have had a cow struggling to calve, a tractor that had broken down or a fence that needed repairing. But it's not just about the Sabbath, it's about our Christian lifestyle.

When I read the four Gospels, I don't only read about Jesus' sermons. What is more important is His lifestyle: He healed the sick, set the captives free, defended the widows and stretched out His hand to the downtrodden. He lived a life of faith.

It's our lifestyle that the world wants to see; let us always be mindful of this.

The Name above All Names

[Jesus] said to them, "But who do you say that I am?" Simon Peter answered and said, "You are the Christ, the Son of the living God."

~ Matthew 16:15-16

The Bible from Genesis to Revelation confirms that Jesus Christ is God. Jesus says many times, "He who has seen Me has seen the Father" (see John 14:7-9; Matt. 11:27 and 1 John 2:23).

As I travel around the world, I hear many different explanations of who God is and I get very concerned. As Christians we must be cautious, lest we allow things in our lives to become more important than God, idols such as money, status, possessions, sport, social media … the list goes on and on.

If you speak about God, no one is offended; that is, until you mention the Name that is above every other name, the name of Jesus Christ. The demons in hell tremble and the evil one departs, because no evil spirit can handle that Name. The name of Jesus will save you and in fact, you might even have to die for it.

Many of the early saints died a martyr's death for it. Let us never forget the privilege of knowing Jesus as our Lord and Saviour.

Fight the Good Fight

Fight the good fight of faith, lay hold on eternal life, to which you were also called and have confessed the good confession in the presence of many witnesses.

~ 1 Timothy 6:12

As Christians, we need to be tenacious and not give up. Nowhere in the Bible can I find the verse that says, "Come to Jesus and all your problems will disappear." In fact, the Lord says the very opposite in Psalm 34:19, "Many are the afflictions of the righteous, but the LORD delivers him out of them all."

Rocky Marciano is the only heavyweight boxing champion of the world to retire undefeated. He only weighed 85kg, but he had unbelievable tenacity. He could take pain and he refused to stay down.

You can ask any successful boxer and he will tell you that the champion is not necessarily the man who can deliver the biggest punch. The champion is the one who can take a hard punch, go down but always get up again. The battle is not in the head; it's in the heart.

Stand strong and never give up, because if you can remain steadfast, you will have the victory. This is the only way we will defeat every demon in hell that would try to turn us away from Jesus.

Wait on the Lord

"Behold, I lay in Zion a stone for a foundation, a tried stone, a precious cornerstone, a sure foundation; whoever believes will not act hastily."

~ Isaiah 28:16

One of the hallmarks of a true child of God is patience. We as believers need to take our time. We need to be patient and not act hastily.

I remember a time when we had planted a crop of maize, but the rains hadn't come. The sun baked the ground hard and the maize kernels did not have the strength to break through the hard crust on the surface.

Some of our neighbours decided to plough their crop back into the ground and start all over again. I decided not to be hasty, so I took our tractor and what is called a spike harrow (a piece of equipment that leaves small indents in the soil). I drove it at high speed over the hard ground. It just touched the surface and the spikes broke up the crust. Two days later, the rain miraculously arrived. We had a beautiful crop of maize, a joy to behold. My neighbours had to fertilise again and reseed.

Don't be impatient, but trust the Lord in everything; He will not disappoint you. Don't rush into hasty decisions, but rather wait on the Lord to direct you.

Redeemed by God

"I washed you in water; yes, I thoroughly washed off your blood, and I anointed you with oil. You were exceedingly beautiful, and succeeded to royalty. Your fame went out among the nations because of your beauty, for it was perfect through My splendor which I had bestowed on you."

~ Ezekiel 16:9, 13-14

What a tremendous price Father God paid for our salvation, offering up His only Son to be crucified on a cross so that our sins might be forgiven and we might find new life in Him.

It is quite a graphic depiction, but God made us alive again, clothed us with beauty and gave us new opportunities and a new vision.

I can only speak for myself, but this Scripture can apply to every child of God. Were it not for the Lord Jesus Christ, we would have surely died in that open field described in Ezekiel 16. But He picked us up, dusted us off and gave us new life.

The Lord wants to do the same for all people. All you need to do is to accept His grace and lovingkindness and say, "Thank You, Lord. I believe." Then you will be redeemed and can start to live as His son or daughter, a life full of hope and peace.

They Shall Be Saved

[Jesus] said to him, "A certain man gave a great supper and invited many …"

~ Luke 14:16

In Luke 14:16-24, we read of the parable of the great supper. Jesus said that a certain man decided to host a grand dinner and invited many of his friends. At suppertime he sent his servants to tell the people to come as the banquet was ready. But they all began making excuses.

The servant came back and told his master all these things. The master was very angry and said, "Go out quickly into the streets and lanes of the city, and bring in here the poor and the maimed and the lame and the blind" (Luke 14:21). Then the master declared that none of those men he had originally invited would taste the dinner.

I have often heard great preachers being used mightily by God, saying that they don't believe they were God's first choice. The Lord has a habit of using people who appear to be unimportant.

Romans 10:13 declares, "Whoever calls on the name of the LORD shall be saved." I called upon the name of the Lord on 18 February 1979 and He "saved a wretch like me." No matter what you've done or how low you've sunk, God will save every person who opens up their heart to Him.

The Bread of Life

"Most assuredly, I say to you, he who believes in Me has everlasting life. I am the bread of life."

~ John 6:47-48

What you eat is what you become. If we eat worldly food, like bitterness, impurity, lust, gossip, immorality, hatred, racialism, greed and self-centredness, then we will become exactly like that. But if we eat of the Bread of Life, we will become spiritually pure and holy.

It is vitally important that we eat the right food if we want to live a long life, both physically and spiritually. We need to eat wholesome spiritual food so that we might develop a strong spiritual physique that will be able to withstand any trial.

I think especially of my grandchildren. It is so important that they receive the Bread of Life. Then, when they grow up and go out into the world, they will be able to stand firm because of the "good food" they have been eating and digesting for many years.

Let us eat the Bread of Life so that we will be ready for any trial or battle we have to face. Remember the words of our Lord: "I am the bread of life. He who comes to Me shall never hunger, and he who believes in Me shall never thirst" (John 6:35).

Give What You Have to Jesus

As a partridge that broods but does not hatch, so is he who gets riches, but not by right; it will leave him in the midst of his days, and at his end he will be a fool.

~ Jeremiah 17:11

We know the story of the foolish farmer who had a wonderful crop and decided he was going to build a bigger barn. Then he was going to eat, drink and be merry. The Lord said to him in Luke 12:20, "Fool! This night your soul will be required of you."

Contrary to this is the beautiful story of the woman in Bethany, who took a flask of very costly fragrant oil and poured it over Jesus' head. Some of the disciples criticised her, saying the oil could have been sold and the money given to the poor (see Mark 14:3-5).

Jesus rebuked them and said in verses 6 and 9, "Why do you trouble her? Assuredly, I say to you, wherever this Gospel is preached in the whole world, what this woman has done will also be told as a memorial to her."

That is an example of a woman who took what she had and gave it to Jesus. Let us not waste our time, or our money on dishonest gain, but rather let's use our blessings for the furtherance of the Kingdom of God.

Give Me Jesus

"The heart is deceitful above all things, and desperately wicked; who can know it? I, the LORD, search the heart, I test the mind, even to give every man according to his ways, according to the fruit of his doings."

~ Jeremiah 17:9-10

How often have you seen and heard of people who are extremely intelligent but whose hearts are wicked? The Lord is more interested in our hearts than our heads. That is why it is so important for us to educate our children about the heart of God first and foremost and then educate them about the things of this world.

One day when we stand before the Lord Jesus Christ, He will not be so concerned about our qualifications. He will be concerned about our hearts for Him, for the poor, the needy and those who need love.

There are so many conferences being held daily in the world and most CEOs of large companies are forever sitting in meetings and receiving information, so much so that they can hardly digest it in their minds.

When they come to church on a Sunday morning, they do not want another lecture or conference; they want Jesus Christ and Him alone. Let us aim to do the same.

Open Your Mouth Wide

"I am the LORD your God … open your mouth wide, and I will fill it."

~ Psalm 81:10

This is what the Lord is saying to those of us who are slow of speech, who would love to be preachers of the Gospel but feel we are not eloquent or educated enough, or we do not have the right personality or character.

All these things are worldly standards, however, and the Lord Jesus Christ does not operate by worldly standards. He has a habit of taking nobodies and using them to perform mighty feats for Him.

Moses, one of the greatest leaders the world has ever seen led an entire nation for 40 years. Yet, when God said to him to go to Pharaoh and tell him to let God's people go, Moses was reluctant. He said, "I am slow of speech and slow of tongue" (Exod. 4:10). The Lord replied, "I will be with your mouth and teach you what you shall say" (Exod. 4:12).

Let us speak out boldly for the King, because He has promised us that He Himself will fill our mouths with words that will encourage, heal, set free and give hope to those who are suffering.

A Faithful Witness

He who is the faithful witness to all these things says, "Yes, I am coming soon!" Amen! Come, Lord Jesus!

~ Revelation 22:20 NLT

While jogging very early one morning, the brightness of the moon lit up my path beautifully!

That is exactly how you and I are supposed to live, to be reflections of Jesus Christ to a very dark world. Psalm 89:37 says that the moon is a faithful witness in the sky. It is the witness of the sun, which in the very early morning is yet unseen.

We are Jesus' faithful witnesses because there are many, many folks who do not know Him yet. So when they see you and me live and act and going about our daily business, we should be faithful reflections of Jesus. Colossians 1:27 says that we can shine brightly to others in a dark world because of "Christ in you, the hope of glory."

Allow the Holy Spirit to come into your life. Be more like Jesus. In the end it is not so much what you say that will make a difference, but who you are and how you choose to live your life.

The moon is like a faithful witness in the sky. It bears proof of the sun, which has not come up yet. But will surely rise again.

To Know Him

Those who are wise shall shine like the brightness of the firmament, and those who turn many to righteousness like the stars forever and ever.

~ Daniel 12:3

A person who is intent on leading people to Jesus Christ is someone who is very wise and who is not wasting any time on this earth. I only have one regret in life and that is that it took me so long to realise my true calling.

There is nothing in my heart that gives me more joy than to see a broken, lost soul find Jesus Christ and in an instant be restored to the person God meant them to be. It is truly the greatest miracle on earth.

When I travel, I always take Gospel tracts and a beautiful little book called *Starting the Journey* with me on the aeroplane. I don't always have the opportunity to have a good chat with someone I meet on board. But what I *can* do is pray with them.

We never know where a person is in terms of their situation in life when we meet them. Sometimes they are laughing, sometimes they are cursing, but often it is just a front. Deep down in their hearts they are crying out for the living God. He created us with that purpose in mind: to know Him more (see Phil. 3:10).

Speak the Truth

Putting away lying, "Let each one of you speak truth with his neighbor," for we are members of one another.

~ Ephesians 4:25

If we exaggerate a story we tell others, it is actually a form of lying. We need to tell the truth as it is. You remember the saying that if you are a liar, you have to have a good memory because you have to remember the lies you told, and to whom!

When a person is looking unwell, don't tell them they are looking fine, because they know better. Most people would prefer that you tell them the truth; then they can deal with the situation. The problem is that when you tell a lie once, people don't trust you after that. No matter how clever you might be, once you have told a lie or spread gossip, you are not to be trusted.

If you tell the truth, sometimes people won't like it and you might even be condemned by society for it, but the truth has a way of always proving itself. Jesus says in John 17:17, "Sanctify them by Your truth. Your word is truth."

It's the truth that sets us free, not lies (see John 8:32). We need to always tell the truth in love. Be honest and forthright (yet gentle) and God will promote you every single time.

Trust in God Alone

Command those who are rich in this present age not to be haughty, nor to trust in uncertain riches but in the living God, who gives us richly all things to enjoy. Let them do good, that they be rich in good works, ready to give, willing to share.

~ 1 Timothy 6:17-18

Are you putting your trust in your finances, in your talents and in your abilities, or are you putting your trust in God? You will recall the saying, "Either you manage your money, or your money manages you." You and I have to ask ourselves an important question: How much is enough?

Remember, we are sojourners in this world. We are not here for very long, so if God has blessed us financially, let us use it for the Kingdom. This is not an easy task. When you don't have much, then money may not mean so much; but when you have a lot and you've worked hard to earn it, it's another story to simply give it away.

I don't think it is money itself that is the problem; it is the love of money that is the root of all evil (see 1 Tim. 6:10). Let us choose to be generous, because God gave it to us in the first place. Let us put our trust in Him alone!

Yes, He's Coming Back!

"You now have sorrow; but I will see you again and your heart will rejoice, and your joy no one will take from you."

~ John 16:22

What an incredibly joyous day Jesus' return is going to be! When the Lord appears in all His glory, it is going to be a momentous occasion. It will be greater than any coronation of any queen or king in the history of the world.

All our past blessings are going to be a mere foretaste of what is still coming for you and me. Therefore, we need to be full of courage, stand fast and at all costs never deny the Lord, because there will be questions He will ask us when He comes back. Will He find a faithful people?

God forbid that we should be found wanting when Christ returns. Remember, He is coming as a thief in the night, so we will not know the hour or the day (see Matt. 24:36, 1 Thess. 5:2). Until we hear the trumpet sound and He comes riding that white stallion (see Rev. 6:2), we must continue His work on earth.

It will be a sight that you and I have been waiting for all our lives, and not only us but all those generations that have gone before us.

Keep Your Eyes Fixed on Jesus

I, therefore, the prisoner of the Lord, beseech you to walk worthy of the calling with which you were called.

~ Ephesians 4:1

Proverbs 4:25-27 tells us, "Let your eyes look straight ahead, and your eyelids look right before you. Ponder the path of your feet, and let all your ways be established. Do not turn to the right or the left; remove your foot from evil."

This reminds me of the book *The Pilgrim's Progress*. Christian is on his way to the celestial city (Heaven). On his journey, he comes across different people who try to put him off. Nevertheless, he keeps to the road he is walking.

We too need to keep our eyes fixed on the road, not looking around and becoming distracted. We need to keep our eyes fixed on Jesus. If we don't, we will lose our way.

We do not have time on this earth to end up in a cul-de-sac. I really believe that Jesus Christ is coming very soon. So keep focused on the journey that God has called you to. Walk this path with all of your heart, as today's Scripture tells us, and do not look behind, and by His grace we will make it to the celestial city.

The Harvest Is Now

The harvest is past, the summer is ended, and we are not saved!

~ Jeremiah 8:20

There is a time to preach the Gospel of Jesus Christ and that time is *now*; we need to do it with all of our hearts, because the opportunities are passing by very quickly and the hope of rescue is growing thin. Do not put off for tomorrow what you can do today; sow your seed and tell others about Jesus, because you don't know whether you will see that person again.

It is so sad when you have known someone for a long time, but you never had the courage to tell them that they need to be born again. Then you hear they have passed away, and death is final. Let us redeem the time; let us use every opportunity to tell people about eternal life and salvation in Jesus Christ.

You might think that people will ridicule you if you share the salvation message with them. That is more than possible, but you have an obligation to at least give them a chance to accept Jesus Christ. The worst that can happen is they slam the door in your face.

However, in most cases they will gladly accept Jesus. It is indeed a noble thing to lead a soul to Christ.

In the Beginning

For since the creation of the world His invisible attributes are clearly seen, being understood by the things that are made, even His eternal power and Godhead, so that they are without excuse.

~ Romans 1:20

We need to ask ourselves a serious question: How did it all begin? Who or what created the world? There's got to be a reason for creation. It cannot just happen spontaneously.

John 1:1-4 says, "In the beginning was the Word, and the Word was with God, and the Word was God. He was in the beginning with God. All things were made through Him, and without Him nothing was made that was made. In Him was life, and the life was the light of men."

We as believers have a definite answer to the creation of the world and it makes perfectly good sense: The world was created by God.

We ought to make Jesus Christ our sole reason for living, because without Him there is nothing and in Him is everything. The Gospel is quite simple and yet at the same time profound. You don't have to be a scientist to understand it. We need to continue to believe that Jesus Christ is the Word and in the beginning was the Word, and that one day all mysteries will be revealed.

The Attitude of the Heart

"Assuredly, I say to you that this poor widow has put in more than all those who have given to the treasury; for they all put in out of their abundance, but she out of her poverty put in all that she had, her whole livelihood."

~ Mark 12:43-44

Attitude is so very important when it comes to giving to God. God does not want you to give to Him with a heart of reluctance (see 2 Cor. 9:7).

In my travels, especially in central Africa, I've had the privilege of staying in many a small hut, where the bathroom consists of a basin, placed very carefully and lovingly on top of some rocks where one can wash. My meal often consists of a bowl of maize meal and maybe a small portion of fish, and that is it. But it is given with such love that it is a great honour to be part of such a humble meal.

It is not what you have, or even the amount you give; it is the heart with which you give it and that is what touches the heart of God.

Mark 8:36 reminds us, "What will it profit a man if he gains the whole world, and loses his own soul?" Let us be mindful of this when we give.

Nothing Is Too Difficult for God

God is not a man, that He should lie, nor a son of man, that
He should repent. Has He said, and will He not do? Or has
He spoken, and will He not make it good?

~ Numbers 23:19

God will never break a covenant. When He says
something, He means it. Genesis 17:1-2 states,
"When Abram was ninety-nine years old, the LORD
appeared to Abram and said to him, 'I am Almighty God;
walk before Me and be blameless. And I will make My
covenant between Me and you, and will multiply you
exceedingly.'"

When God says something, He means it. Abraham was
almost 100 years old, as was his wife, and yet he had
a promise that he would have more children than the
stars in the sky.

To mortal eyes, by the time Abraham and his wife were
in their nineties, it looked like God had broken His
covenant. Yet, God gave Abraham and Sarah a beautiful
son named Isaac.

If the Lord makes a promise, He keeps it. Sometimes
you and I break our side of the covenant, because of
fear, faithlessness or pressure. It doesn't matter how
impossible it may seem, we need to stand on God's
word. Nothing is too difficult for our omniscient God.

Heavenly Humility

"And it shall be, in that day," says the LORD, "That you will call Me 'My Husband,' and no longer call Me 'My Master,' for I will take from her mouth the names of the Baals, and they shall be remembered by their name no more."

~ Hosea 2:16-17

What a beautiful reason to love the Lord Jesus. He says that He will no longer be called Master but a loving husband, not that we will respect Him any less; in fact, we will love and honour Him more.

Grace has cast out all fear and love has been implanted in our hearts. That is why Sunday is a day of great delight to the believer and not a day of weariness. Prayer is a pleasure and not a tedious task, while worshipping Jesus feels like a holiday. To obey Him is like being in Heaven, and to give money to the Kingdom is a privilege and an honour. When I am going about the work of the Lord, my mouth is full of praise and my heart overflows with great love.

There is no leader or king who has ever been as humble as our loving Lord Jesus; Someone who was willing to take a basin and a towel and wash the dirty feet of His disciples.

Surely we need to do the same and demonstrate humble love to all people.

The Storms of Life

The righteous cry out, and the LORD hears, and delivers them out of all their troubles.

~ Psalm 34:17

From time to time we have the most incredible storms on our farm in KwaZulu-Natal. The wind blows with such velocity that large branches break off the trees and we think the roof of our house is going to blow off. We get up early the next morning and I hear the birds singing, and I think, *Lord Jesus, how is it that the birds are singing after such a storm*?

Many of us sometimes think that with the storms we go through, we will never survive because they are so destructive. Maybe you have lost a loved one and you think you will never be able to face another day.

Perhaps your business has gone under and you have had to declare bankruptcy. Maybe you have a member of your family who has disappointed you. You may feel that it is all too much and you can't take it any longer.

The truth of the matter is: you can! In fact, you can take a lot more than you realise. You just need to keep your head up and remain close to Jesus; He will see you through.

Sow in Abundance

The love of money is a root of all kinds of evil, for which some have strayed from the faith in their greediness, and pierced themselves through with many sorrows.

~ 1 Timothy 6:10

As a farmer, I know that you only harvest what you sow. If you don't sow any seed, or you don't sow it in abundance, then you won't reap an abundant crop. The same can be said of money.

I know many rich, wealthy and successful businessmen who are among the most generous people I've ever met in my life. They do it for the Lord and they usually prefer to remain anonymous.

Many people in our country are successful because they operate their businesses according to God's biblical principles and that is why God blesses them so abundantly. Whatever they put their hand to seems to turn to gold, but you'll find that they take care of the poor and the needy, the widows and the orphans. They also faithfully tithe their 10%. I've had the privilege of meeting some very unselfish and honourable people over the years.

May God bless you as you use that which He has given to you to further the Kingdom of Heaven here on earth.

Being Born Again

Jesus answered and said to him, "Most assuredly, I say to you, unless one is born again, he cannot see the kingdom of God."

~ John 3:3

Nicodemus came to Jesus by night because he didn't want anyone to see him since he was a member of the Sanhedrin, the ruling elders of Israel. He wanted to ask Jesus about eternity.

He was shocked by what He had to say. Nicodemus asked, "How can a man be born when he is old? Can he enter a second time into his mother's womb and be born?" (John 3:4). Jesus replied, "I say to you, unless one is born of water and the Spirit, he cannot enter the kingdom of God" (John 3:5).

What does it mean to be born again? It means to give your life wholly to Jesus and to make a clean start. Each one of us needs to accept Jesus Christ personally as our Lord and Saviour.

When you meet the Lord and your relationship with Him begins, it just continues to grow. It doesn't matter what you have done in this world, if you don't know Jesus Christ, you will not have that incredible peace.

Let us not leave the decision until it is too late, for the Bible says that God "desires all men to be saved and to come to the knowledge of the truth" (1 Tim. 2:4).

A Heart Filled with Gratitude

"The older brother was angry and wouldn't go in. His father came out and begged him."

~ Luke 15:28 NLT

Jealousy, envy and anger can deprive us of so much good. We need to be so careful that we don't become envious of the way in which God blesses someone else.

I know one very dear friend of mine who farms over-seas who has sons and a daughter. His daughter was extremely upset when he did not leave her any land. What he did leave her was money, but she didn't seem to understand that she had the equivalent inheritance, only of a different kind.

No one is entitled to anything more than a good education and a decent upbringing. All the rest that comes is purely a gift and so often young people don't understand that. They think an inheritance is auto-matic and that they need to receive the exact same amount as the others. That is not the case. Every child is blessed by their father and mother according to what they feel is fair.

We need to understand that the Lord has given us eternal life for free and we in turn need to be grateful for every single thing we receive from God.

August

To each one of us grace was given according to the measure of Christ's gift.

~ Ephesians 4:7 ~

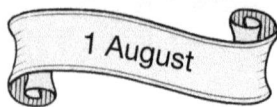

A True Friend

There are "friends" who destroy each other, but a real friend sticks closer than a brother.

~ Proverbs 18:24 NLT

A true friend is one that you can call upon at any time of the day or night. That friend sometimes knows you better than you know yourself. They can put up with all your moods, the highs and lows, and still be there for you. They always see the best in you, believe in you and pray for you!

I have known the Lord intimately for many years now. In my darkest hour, when no one else could help me, my Friend was there. He literally pulled me out of the miry pit!

This Friend of mine calms the storms in my life. He also patiently waits for me every single day – even when I am sometimes late for our appointment. We go jogging together early in the mornings and as strong and fit as He is, He never leaves me behind. He is always right beside me!

Really get to know Him more intimately and spend time with Him, because you need Him desperately. His name is Jesus! And you can also contact Him on Jeremiah 33:3, "Call to Me, and I will answer you, and show you great and mighty things, which you do not know."

I Will Believe It When I See It

"Unless I see in His hands the print of the nails, and put my finger into the print of the nails, and put my hand into His side, I will not believe."

~ John 20:25

Seeing is believing. That was basically what Thomas said to the disciples when they told him that Jesus had risen from the dead (see John 20:24-29).

I think that it really hurts God when we question His promises over our lives. Clear promises from Scripture that tell us, "I will never leave you nor forsake you," (Heb. 13:5) and still we doubt.

If there is one great attribute of God that I have learned in my walk with Him, it is that He is faithful and that we can always trust Him and His promises to us.

When we regularly spend time with Jesus, our faith is strengthened. However, when we get sidetracked by the cares of this world, our faith starts to wane. Jesus said, "Blessed are those who have not seen and yet have believed" (John 20:29). Faith comes by hearing, and hearing by the Word of God (see Rom. 10:17).

The Greatest Miracle

"Yes," says the LORD, "I will do mighty miracles for you, like those I did when I rescued you from slavery in Egypt."

~ Micah 7:15 NLT

A miracle is an object of wonder, or an extraordinary and welcome event that is not explainable by natural or scientific laws attributed to a divine agency.

The greatest miracle that has ever been performed in this world is the resurrection of our Saviour and Lord Jesus Christ! The tomb is empty. There are no bones or relics left there. I have been there and seen the tomb with my own eyes.

Romans 8:11 says, "But if the Spirit of Him who raised Jesus from the dead dwells in you, He who raised Christ from the dead will also give life to your mortal bodies through His Spirit who dwells in you." What an incredible promise and by faith we need to embrace this word from God as we face life's challenges.

You and I need to believe in miracles like never before. Jesus is alive. What an incredible truth to hold on to, therefore we shall not be fearful nor afraid.

What Is Truth?

"Lord, I believe; help my unbelief!"

~ Mark 9:24

Pontius Pilate asked the Son of God, "What is truth?" This same question that the Roman governor asked Jesus some 2000 years ago, is still being asked to this very day.

God's sovereign Word is truth and this Word will set us free. But it will also condemn us. Free if we believe it and condemned if we don't believe. We are in this world, but we are not part of this world just as our Redeemer was not part of this world (see John 17:16).

We shouldn't feel rejected or be concerned about not being popular when the world shuns us simply because we will not compromise God's Holy Word.

Do you believe in Him and trust in Him? Is your name written in the Lamb's Book of Life because you are a believer?

You see, Jesus did not have to defend Himself because He had absolutely nothing to hide. His lifestyle spoke volumes. He took care of the widows and orphans. He performed miracles, signs and wonders. He spoke prophetic words. Let us follow His example. Get down on your knees and say, "Lord, we believe in You. We will not doubt You. We will trust You to meet our needs."

Life's Real Purpose

Know that the LORD, He is God; it is He who has made us, and not we ourselves; we are His people and the sheep of His pasture.

~ Psalm 100:3

When you ask someone what they really desire in life they will probably say something like, "I want to be happy, successful and at peace!"

You can try all you want to attain all those blessings but they will allude you, simply because they are merely by-products of what we receive when we discover our true purpose in life.

The chief end of man is to glorify God and to enjoy Him forever. When we live according to those two principles, then we will find peace and contentment.

Jesus said, "'You shall love the LORD your God with all your heart, with all your soul, and with all your mind.' This is the first and great commandment. And the second is like it: 'You shall love your neighbor as yourself'" (Matt. 22:37-39).

When we obey these two commandments, then the things that we seek will be ours. Mark Twain said, "The two most important days in your life are the day you are born and the day you find out why." If you don't have a purpose in life, ask God to show it to you. It doesn't have to be a massive vision; start small and God will promote you when the time is right.

Too Busy …

We are merely moving shadows, and all our busy rushing ends in nothing.

~ Psalm 39:6 NLT

Often we become so busy that we start to lose heart for people – for important occasions, for individuals and their needs. We get into a survival mode and in the process we start to push people aside, especially the old, the infirm and the handicapped, in order to get the job done.

The extreme busyness of our lives causes our hearts to become so seared that we lose personal touch with people and our sensitive heart dies. Too often we forget to take time out to smell the roses.

Jesus must have realised that this was starting to happen to His disciples. He said to them in Mark 6:31, "'Come aside by yourselves to a deserted place and rest a while.' For there were many coming and going, and they did not even have time to eat."

Let's take a close look at our lives and ask ourselves an honest question: Are we too busy? What are we going to do about it? Because if we do not take immediate action on this warning from God, we will lose touch with those who are nearest and dearest to us.

A Miracle-Working God

Jesus spoke to them, saying, "Be of good cheer! It is I; do not be afraid."

~ Matthew 14:27

I believe that one genuine miracle equals a thousand sermons. If you only open your eyes, you will see miracles happening around you all the time.

Once a private plane was to fly me to the North West Province of our beloved South Africa for a Mighty Men conference. However, the weatherman stated very clearly that the mist would be down to the ground and the plane would not be able to land.

Just before 4 A.M. on the day, I walked outside and the stars were shining brightly. No mist in sight. The plane arrived on time for our appointment. Then I got up again at 4 A.M. the next day and the mist was thick and right down to the ground. There was no way that a plane could fly. It was no coincidence, it was a miracle!

Start seeing the miracles God puts in your life every day and thank Him for each one. You will be pleasantly surprised just how closely God is walking with you. It will drastically increase your faith.

Choose Wisely

Choose for yourselves this day whom you will serve … But as for me and my house, we will serve the LORD.

~ Joshua 24:15

Life is a choice. You can choose to live an abundant life just as Jesus promised in John 10:10, or you can choose death if you follow after and believe the lies of the devil.

Jesus gave us a free will so that we can choose for ourselves – life or death. We have no one to blame but ourselves if we choose to walk away from God and life! Our circumstances, finances, relationships, health or current situation cannot be blamed. It is a decision we take on our own. Job said, "Though He slay me, yet will I trust Him" (Job 13:15). God can certainly work with such a man.

Which reminds me of the story of Shadrach, Meshach and Abednego. They were told to choose death or life, serve Nebuchadnezzar or die in the furnace. Their response was, "Let it be known to you, O king, that we do not serve your gods, nor will we worship the gold image which you have set up" (Dan. 3:18).

All three of them were thrown into a blazing furnace but did not perish. Make the right decision today!

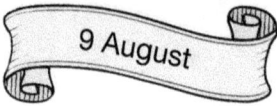

The Door

Jesus said to him, "I am the way, the truth, and the life. No one comes to the Father except through Me."

~ John 14:6

There is no other way into God's Kingdom but through the door and Jesus tells us very clearly that He alone is that door.

The shepherds of old would construct an enclosure of thorn branches at night to keep their flock of sheep protected from wild animals. The door to that enclosure would be the shepherd himself. He would sleep across the opening so that anything going out or coming in would have to pass through him.

We read in John 10:9, "I am the door. If anyone enters by Me, he will be saved, and will go in and out and find pasture."

There is no other way to find eternal life, peace and security, but by and through the Son of God, Jesus. He is the Good Shepherd who will do anything for His flock. Jesus said very clearly that He is the only way. There is no other entrance into Heaven, except by Him.

You and I have an obligation today – to show lost sheep the way to Jesus. We have to guide them to enter through the door that will lead them safely home.

Life Is Not Fair

He is the Rock, His work is perfect; for all His ways are justice, a God of truth and without injustice; righteous and upright is He.

~ Deuteronomy 32:4

Turn on the TV and watch the news. The first thing one realises is the injustice and the lack of fairness that is running rampant in our poor, sick world. Furthermore, it always seems to be the poor, innocent citizen who is minding his own business, trying to make ends meet, that is constantly feeling the brunt of it all.

How do we handle it when life seems unfair? When governments make decisions that literally affect multitudes of innocent defenceless women and children? There is only one Man we can turn to for solace, comfort and strength; His name is Jesus Christ – the very Son of the living God!

He said that in Him we shall have peace. In this world we are going to have tribulation. But you and I must be of good cheer, because He, Jesus, has overcome the world on our behalf (see John 16:33).

We live in an imperfect world and things will not always go our way, but God loves us and will redeem us in the end.

Count Your Blessings

I will mention the lovingkindnesses of the LORD and the praises of the LORD, according to all that the LORD has bestowed on us.

~ Isaiah 63:7

Are you feeling down today? Then how about counting all the good things Jesus has done for you. Like the day He rescued you from the dark pit of despondency, cleaned you off and gave you new life. Remember how He forgave all of your sins? How He helped you find a job, restored your tarnished reputation and set you free from addiction.

If you're feeling downhearted right now, ask yourself: Has Jesus not set me free from such situations in the past? Of course He has, many times, and He will do it again if you will just let Him.

Like David of old, speak to your soul in the words of Psalm 42:5, "Why are you cast down, O my soul? And why are you disquieted within me? Hope in God, for I shall yet praise Him."

It is a new day, a new beginning and He will not fail us nor disappoint us. Go in faith and Jesus shall see us through (see Phil. 1:6).

The God of the Living

"He is not the God of the dead, but the God of the living."
~ Mark 12:27

As I was writing today's reading, I was on cloud nine because the previous day at a prayer meeting in Johannesburg, I encountered the God of the living.

I'm convinced that Jesus is alive and moving as miraculously today as ever. "Jesus Christ is the same yesterday, today and forever" (Heb. 13:8).

We saw multitudes of people coming to hear God's Word. Why, you ask? Because people are longing to quench the thirst deep within their souls. And Jesus is alive and very active in these dark days to be the Living Water to weary souls.

How often do I have the privilege of seeing crowds come together in His name and over again He meets all their needs. It is time to tell this sick and depressed world that He is alive and well and that He is returning very soon.

Jesus said of His Father, "He is not the God of the dead, but of the living" (Luke 20:38). God bless you today as you put all your trust in the miracle-working Jesus!

Tell People About Jesus

"Go therefore and make disciples of all the nations, baptizing them in the name of the Father and of the Son and of the Holy Spirit."

~ Matthew 28:19

God reveals in John 4:39-42 that the Samaritan woman, after having spoken with Jesus at the well, went into town and told everyone that she had met a stranger who told her everything about her past.

Many of the inhabitants of the town believed that Jesus was the Messiah because of her miraculous testimony. All you and I have to do for the Kingdom is to introduce people to Jesus and He will do the rest.

In John 4:42, we see the people told the Samaritan woman: "Now we believe … for we ourselves have heard Him and we know that this is indeed the Christ, the Savior of the world."

The Samaritan woman of ill repute was neither an evangelist, nor a famous preacher and yet because of her personal testimony the whole town went to listen to Jesus and believed.

Let's go out today into a broken, hurting world and tell precious souls what the Son of God has done for us. Jesus will do the rest.

Think Before You Speak

For the Scriptures say, "If you want to enjoy life and see many happy days, keep your tongue from speaking evil and your lips from telling lies."

~ 1 Peter 3:10 NLT

We really need to measure our words. The golden rule still applies: If you haven't got anything good to say, then don't say anything at all.

Count to ten before you let your tongue loose and then later regret what you have said. Many relationships end because of thoughtless words. Rather exercise love, self-control and grace, and save a friendship!

The more we speak the more often we incriminate ourselves and get ourselves into trouble. We are to let our lives speak for us. Yes indeed, there is a time to speak up and there is a time to keep quiet, but the Holy Spirit Himself will tell us when that time is.

Today when you go out, remember that when Jesus was falsely accused by the government and by the church, He never said a word. His actions redeemed Him. Go out today and be the salt of the world. Be Jesus to people who are in tremendous need. Love people. Words are cheap; actions speak much louder.

Ask yourself one question before you speak: What would Jesus do? Then go ahead and do exactly that.

Far Above Rubies

Who can find a virtuous wife? For her worth is far above rubies.

~ Proverbs 31:10

To the husbands I'm saying today: We need to honour and love our wives much more than we do, and most of all appreciate them as a true gift from God.

We need to listen to their godly counsel more than we do to other people. They have no ulterior motives, they only have the well-being of their families at heart and that's why they tell us the truth.

Unlike many others, they do not tell us what we want to hear, but rather what is good for us. They stick with us when the going is good and when the going gets tough. We need to love and appreciate the women in our lives a whole lot more.

If a woman stands in her husband's corner that man – irrespective of size or stature – will knock out the heavyweight boxing champion of the world with no problem at all.

God created us to be in close relationship with one another. In the book of Ecclesiastes, the writer says two people are better off than one because they can help each other succeed (see Eccles. 4:9-10). If one person falls, the other can reach out and help him. But someone who falls alone is in real trouble.

A Life of Song

... singing with grace in your hearts to the Lord.

~ Colossians 3:16

The Master challenged me and spoke to my heart with today's Scripture verse.

You might very well think that you have nothing to be joyful about. You've just lost a loved one, your wife left you or your business is on the verge of bankruptcy ... Then Jesus says to you today, "I will never leave you nor forsake you" (Heb. 13:5).

Today we have a choice to make: Are we going to live this day by sight or by faith? Remember it's the joy of the Lord that will give you the strength to carry on (see Neh. 8:10). In fact, singing and walking in joy and even laughing is like good medicine (see Prov. 17:22).

No matter how depressed you might be feeling today, praise the Lord, because there is power in praise. It is like medicine for the body. Jesus praised His Father before He delivered Lazarus from the tomb. The good farmer praises God while he's planting the seed for a harvest that is yet to be seen or reaped.

God honours faith and He honours those who praise Him. Praise His name today, because He is worthy to be praised. Let us sing for joy, for Jesus is on His way.

My Dearest Companion

Your word is a lamp to my feet and a light to my path.
~ Psalm 119:105

When I have been at my absolute lowest, my faithful Friend has been there for me. When I needed godly counsel, my dearest Companion directed me, wiped my tears away and healed my broken heart in times of great pain and personal tragedy. When I felt extremely lonely, I found solace and comfort, for my rock-solid Guide was there for me!

Who is this Friend? It is the Bible of course and without it I could not live another day.

The Bible is Jesus in written form. "In the beginning was the Word, and the Word was with God, and the Word was God" (John 1:1). So the next time someone says to you, "Show me this Jesus you're always talking about," give him a Bible!

My friend, faith comes by hearing and hearing by the Word of God (see Rom. 10:17). Many people ask me to pray that God would increase their faith. I always say that I won't pray for God to increase their faith; instead I will pray for them to hunger after the Word of God and to read and believe the Bible. The more time you spend with the Word of God, the greater your faith will become.

Encourage One Another

So encourage each other and build each other up, just as you are already doing.

~ 1 Thessalonians 5:11

A knife is an important tool. I find myself not feeling fully dressed if I go out onto the farm without a knife. It's very handy. The emphasis of course is on the knife being *sharp*! There is nothing worse than trying to work with a dull blade. A good farmer's knife will always be well-oiled and razor sharp.

It is the same in the Kingdom of God. We as His children are to sharpen each other in love. To sharpen iron you need a file or a grindstone. This process can be painful, but always worthwhile in the end.

I need to encourage you to be careful, first of all, of the company you keep; secondly, of the media you surround yourself with; and thirdly, of the conversations you have with others, because they could tarnish and taint your character and personality.

Let us truly show our love for one another through a gentle correction and an encouraging word of wisdom, so that we can keep each other sharp for the work of the Lord Jesus.

Do Not Grow Weary

But as for you, brethren, do not grow weary in doing good.
~ 2 Thessalonians 3:13

The Lord Jesus laid upon my heart Galatians 6:9, "Let us not grow weary while doing good, for in due season we shall reap if we do not lose heart."

We cannot afford to go back to the bondage of sin. We have been set free from the oppression of the devil.

As children of God we are set free from hatred, fear, condemnation and eternal death. John 10:10 says, "The thief does not come except to steal, and to kill, and to destroy. I have come that they may have life, and that they may have it more abundantly."

We need to be very careful that the evil one does not rob us of that joy and freedom we have in Christ by distracting us with the challenges we face.

We will never agree with, nor turn a blind eye to lawlessness, or the murder of innocent people. Justice must take its rightful course and we as God-fearing citizens should do everything we can to assist. But we can never take the law into our own hands.

The Battle Against Darkness

So they said, "Believe on the Lord Jesus Christ, and you will be saved, you and your household."

~ Acts 16:31

How are we as believers to face the future in a society that seems to disregard human life?

Well, we need to provide for our families on every front, protecting them physically and spiritually, feeding them, clothing them and caring for their needs. Jesus says a person that does not take care of their own household is worse than an unbeliever (see 1 Tim. 5:8). Nowhere in the Bible does Jesus allow a person to become slack in their responsibility towards their own household.

The only way we can fulfil the responsibilities the Lord has given us is through God's Holy Word, the Bible, and prayer. God will bless and protect you and your loved ones as you put your ultimate trust in Him.

If you have a spouse and children, take time out to spend with them. If not, focus on your closest relationships and the state of your personal affairs. God has called you to minister to your household first, whoever that may be.

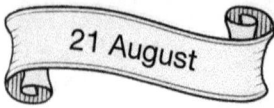

Redemption Is Yours

"Greater love has no one than this, than to lay down one's life for his friends."

~ John 15:13

Having been asked to speak on the subject of redemption at a church's 25th anniversary, I did some research and was truly blessed by this word. Psalm 49:7 (NLT) says, "Yet they cannot redeem themselves from death by paying a ransom to God." In other words, no man can redeem the life of another, for the cost is just too great.

Redemption means something or someone that saves someone from error or evil. We have such a Person and His name is Jesus. He alone is the Redeemer of this world. Jesus is God's only provision for man's sin. Only through Him can we know God personally and be forgiven.

Salvation is a free gift we receive through Jesus' sacrifice on the cross. When we're saved, we can be confident that Jesus' work has wiped out our sin so He can walk with us and take care of us in a loving, close relationship.

There is no self-rescue. So today, call upon the name of our Redeemer, Jesus. He will save you from any error and evil that the devil attempts to bring across your path.

Beware of False Prophets

Because of these teachers, the way of truth will be slandered.

~ 2 Peter 2:2 NLT

While reading 2 Peter 2:1-3, I felt the Holy Spirit remind me to be very careful of some so-called prophetic words spoken by false prophets in these last days. People are desperate for anything that resembles life, hope, direction and purpose.

We need to really test such prophetic words before we take them seriously. If it lines up with the Bible's teaching, then you can believe it. If it does not, then reject it. As believers, everything we have and everything we are, comes directly from God's Word!

A good example of a false prophetic word is when someone tries to tell you the exact date of Jesus' return. Jesus Himself says that no one knows the date of His Second Coming. Not even He knows. Only the Father knows (see Mark 13:32).

Another telltale sign is that false prophets always try to bring fear into the hearts of the children of God. But because we know and believe in God, they fail miserably. Remember, if it's not in the Bible, do not believe a word of it!

A Safe Place

So we may boldly say: "The LORD is my helper; I will not fear. What can man do to me?"

~ Hebrews 13:6

We received a very touching email a while ago from a dear lady who was obviously quite concerned about the future.

She said that a lot of people were worried about a story that was being circulated around Cape Town. It was about a tsunami that was going to hit the Western Cape. She said that a member of her family had already sold up and moved to Kimberley.

The weapon that the devil is using now more than ever before is fear. However, 2 Timothy 1:7 clearly says, "For God has not given us a spirit of fear, but of power and of love and of a sound mind."

Our advice to the lady was quite simply to stay exactly where she was, unless she received a clear word from the Lord.

Sometimes in my travels overseas, I meet up with fellow South Africans who emigrated. Many of them would return home instantly if they could, but unfortunately they have burned their bridges and do not have the financial means to come back. Only do exactly what God has told you to do. Words from men should only confirm what God has already put in your heart.

The World Belongs to God

"For the world is Mine, and all its fullness."

~ Psalm 50:12

The other day, God showed me very clearly from today's Scripture verse, as well as in Exodus 19:5, that the whole world belongs to Him alone.

In other words, we are not owners of the land or any of its contents, or even our very lives. We are purely managers thereof.

It takes some of the pressure off us in terms of the huge responsibility that we sometimes feel is ours: to perform, to produce and to deliver! You see, that is a direct ploy of the evil one: to get us moving on the treadmill and keep us there until we collapse under worry and work responsibilities.

The good news for you and me today is that everything belongs to Jesus. Even our lives and troubles are His responsibility. As a result, all that we have to do is what He tells us to – nothing more and nothing less.

What liberty, what joy, what peace. Why are we fretting and worrying when it all belongs to Him? And Jesus has never failed us and He never will.

Today, let us enjoy that with which He has entrusted us and leave the ultimate burden of ownership entirely in His gracious hands.

Follow Your Dreams

Now may the Lord direct your hearts into the love of God and into the patience of Christ.

~ 2 Thessalonians 3:5

People often write to me and tell me of the dreams, visions and word they received from God through their quiet times; a calling to fulfil a particular function for the Kingdom and they're looking for some direction.

Time is fast running out. We need to act upon the prompting of the Holy Spirit, then get confirmation of that call through the written Word of God, as well as from trusted fellow believers. And then do it!

Every single man and woman of God has to start somewhere. It requires faith and obedience. Remember, Jesus doesn't only use the sharpest tool in the shed. He uses those who will raise their hand and say, "Lord, all I have are two small fish and five loaves of bread." "That's more than enough," Jesus would answer and then multiply the food to feed a multitude of starving souls (see John 6:9-14).

The Master is calling us to get started and to use what we have. It might only be a stick, like Moses had when he was tending Jethro's sheep, but to God that's more than enough (see Exod. 3).

Walk the Talk

For by grace you have been saved through faith, and that not of yourselves; it is the gift of God, not of works, lest anyone should boast.

~ Ephesians 2:8-9

In Ephesians 4:1, Paul the apostle says that we need to live the life of a believer – not so much talking about it, but actually living it.

It should not be seen as an effort, or even a duty; rather, it should come out of the very pores of our skin. It should come naturally, simply because of who Jesus is in our lives!

The person on the street should be able to come up to us in the supermarket, on the sports field, in the lecture hall, or on the farm and ask us what we have, because they want it too.

It's the peace, the joy, the complete confidence in Jesus, the purpose for living … That is what people in this dying world desperately desire. It cannot be bought.

We shouldn't have to try to do good works for people or persuade them to come to Christ. It should come naturally, yes, spontaneously, because of the presence of Christ in us.

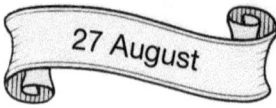

No Drawing Back

Let us hold fast the confession of our hope without wavering, for He who promised is faithful.

~ Hebrews 10:23

Today's Scripture verse is such a beautiful reminder to see us through a hard day, a busy week or month. Jesus tells you and me to hold fast to our faith without doubting, because the Lord is faithful.

This is not the time for us to give up, or to turn our backs on God. We have come so far and we are near the finish line. Hebrews 10:35 states very clearly that we are not to throw away our confidence, which has such a great reward awaiting us. Let us ask Jesus for endurance and let's continue to live by faith (see Rom. 1:17).

Maybe there is something that is really troubling you this morning. Today you can rest assured that God is faithful. Even when your faith level is at its lowest, He is still as faithful as ever. Matthew Henry, a great Christian theologian who lived from 1662 to 1714, said, "When I cannot feel the faith of assurance, I live by the fact of God's faithfulness."

If today we cannot trust in our feeling of faith, we can trust in the faithfulness of God.

Your Debts Are Paid

"I have blotted out, like a thick cloud, your transgressions, and like a cloud, your sins. Return to Me, for I have redeemed you."

~ Isaiah 44:22

Do you know the hymn *"I had a debt I could not pay, He paid the debt He did not owe, I needed someone to wash my sins away"*?

Well, early one morning while I was having my quiet time, Jesus reminded me again of His sole purpose for coming down from His throne room in Heaven … It was to die for our sins, to offer Himself up as a living sacrifice.

In Hebrews 10:5-10, Jesus states no less than twice that He is fully committed to carrying out God's will and to offer Himself up as a living sacrifice for the sins of all the world. What incredible love!

Our hope is in eternal life, not in the here and now. Jesus said that He is going ahead to prepare a place for us (see John 14:2). And we will be there together with our loved ones forever. Death has lost its sting. God bless you and help you to keep looking up; your redemption draws near.

Let us go out to the highways and byways and tell at least three people that our debt is fully paid up and that theirs can be too – if they would simply believe.

God Is Good

How kind the LORD is! How good He is! So merciful, this God of ours!

~ Psalm 116:5 NLT

The Bible tells us very clearly in Hebrews 12:29 that our God is a consuming fire. Our God is a holy God and needs to be shown the utmost respect by His people. He is the God who created Heaven and earth by just speaking the word (see John 1:1-3).

The Lord is a loving Saviour and Lion of Judah. Today, let's love Him and respect Him because He died protecting us from evil; yes, indeed He gave His very life for us. We need to honour Him and give Him first place in our lives and not act disrespectful towards Him!

He is a mighty God and expects us to be holy people too! In fact, He says that without holiness, no man will see Him (see Heb. 12:14). Love Him, enjoy Him. He wants to spend intimate time with you today. But never forget that He is God.

Show God the respect that He deserves and thank Him for His amazing love. The Bible says, "Greater love has no one than this, than to lay down ones life for his friends" (John 15:13).

The Excellence of Wisdom

Does not wisdom cry out, and understanding lift up her voice? Receive my instruction, and not silver, and knowledge rather than choice gold.

~ Proverbs 8:1, 10

Jesus says to us today that we are to seek wisdom before gold or silver. It is the fear of God that is wisdom and the departing from evil that is good understanding (see Job 28:28).

There are just so many different opinions out there today and it can be very confusing to say the least, if not downright scary.

Do I go into business with that person or not? Is it better for me to leave or to stay? To buy or to sell? Should I undergo the operation, or trust God for healing?

At the end of the day, it is actually our decision to make. No one else can do it for us. That is why we need to have regular quiet times each morning, so that Jesus can direct our paths and give us His wisdom through the Bible, prayer and meditation. He will give you direction.

"But seek first the kingdom of God and His righteousness, and all these things shall be added to you" (Matt. 6:33). Go out with confidence and face the new day, knowing that He goes before you.

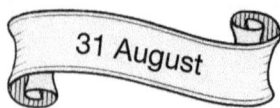

Truth and Mercy

"Blessed are the merciful, for they shall obtain mercy."

~ Matthew 5:7

As I sat quietly in the mountains and watched the sun rise above the majestic peaks on a crisp winter's morning, I felt very close to God. I could almost tangibly hear Him say, "Extend mercy and truth."

It is what people need so desperately at this volatile time we are living in.

Proverbs 3:3 says, "Let not mercy and truth forsake you; bind them around your neck, write them on the tablet of your heart." By doing that, you will find favour with God.

We need to be gentler with one another, speaking the truth in love and mercy. It's only the truth that can set the captive free, but always spoken from a merciful spirit.

The Lord says, "Blessed are the merciful, for they shall obtain mercy" (Matt. 5:7). Today, try to be more compassionate towards that person at your workplace or at home. Remember that God has been extremely merciful towards you. You might think, "It's not fair, I don't deserve this," and you are probably quite right. Neither did Jesus deserve to be crucified for our sins. Yet, He did it gracefully.

September

The Lord Jesus Christ be with your spirit.
Grace be with you.

~ 2 Timothy 4:22 ~

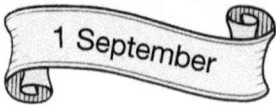

Don't Throw Stones

For by grace you have been saved through faith, and that not of yourselves; it is the gift of God.

~ Ephesians 2:8

Early this morning, while reading my precious Bible, the Lord Jesus spoke to me almost audibly from Titus 3:1-8.

He reminded me very clearly that we are to live lives of peace, gentleness and humility, being very careful not to become harsh and judgemental towards our fellow man. Once we were also foolish, disobedient, followed after self-gratification and lived lives of total self-centeredness! Jesus saved us, gave us new life, forgave our sins and made us into brand new people (see 2 Cor. 5:17). Where would you and I be today without Him?

The Lord says we need to exercise extreme grace towards our fellow man so that they too might find eternal life through Jesus Christ. We must never forget that. Let us exercise that same grace towards others who are struggling and who are trying to follow the right path. The love of Christ that we have today is because we have been reminded by God that it's by grace alone that we have been saved.

Let us repent today and say, "Lord, forgive us. Forgive us for judging others. Thank You for reminding us where we came from. Amen."

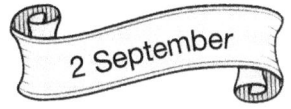

The Small Things

Do not despise these small beginnings, for the LORD rejoices to see the work begin.

~ Zechariah 4:10 NLT

It's the little things in life that can make a big diffe-rence! Things left undone or unsaid can have major repercussions. So let's make sure we leave no "small things" undone today, like telling your wife that you love her. Tell your husband you really appreciate what he's doing for you and your family.

Give your children an encouraging word, especially when they are writing exams. Mend that broken re-lationship today and pay the account that is behind as soon as you can.

I love the Lord so much because He has a habit of choosing the "small things" to confuse the "big things" in this world. The reason He does that is because He doesn't want to share His glory with any man. He knows that when He uses you in that small capacity, when He takes the two fish and five barley loaves, multiplies them and feeds a multitude, no man will take the glory for it. The glory can only belong to God.

Go out today and don't despise small beginnings. We all have to start somewhere. God will take everything that you give Him and multiply it, because He's in the multiplying business.

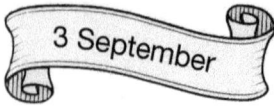

Genuine Faith

I call to remembrance the genuine faith that is in you, which dwelt first in your grandmother Lois and your mother Eunice, and I am persuaded is in you also.

~ 2 Timothy 1:5

In today's verse, Paul remembers the genuine faith that Timothy's mother Eunice and his grandmother Lois had – a genuine faith without fear.

The Bible tells us that God did not give us a spirit of fear, but of power and of love and of a sound mind (see 2 Tim. 1:7).

If it is founded in God's Word, then believe it. God is interested in you and me. He is for us. He wants to give us good things. All He wants us to do is to call upon His name but not just that, calling upon His name in faith.

I have found that the more time I spend talking to God and listening to Him, the more clearly I hear His voice. The more I block out doubt and unbelief, the more peace I have. As a result, I live more by faith and in the power of God.

It is only when we spend time waiting on the Lord in prayer and reading His Word that the Lord gives us the faith we need to accomplish the work He has called us to do.

The Great Mystery

I write so that you may know how you ought to conduct yourself in the house of God, which is the church of the living God, the pillar and ground of the truth.

~ 1 Timothy 3:15

First Timothy 3:14-16 speaks of the great mystery, the mainstay of the faith. It says that God was ...

- manifested in the flesh
- justified in the Spirit
- seen by angels
- preached among the Gentiles
- believed on in the world
- received up in glory.

There is no need for any other proof to confirm that Jesus is indeed "God made flesh," the Messiah.

Why did Jesus choose to humble Himself and come to earth as a human being to be God with us? Why did He leave His home in Heaven to come down to earth to be crucified for sinners? He was prepared to expose Himself to ridicule and punishment so that we might be saved and receive eternal life.

Go out on your own, maybe for a walk in the garden. Think about what the Lord did for you on that eventful night when He was born. His suffering for our sake did not start in the Garden of Gethsemane. His suffering started on the day He was born. All we need to do is believe it!

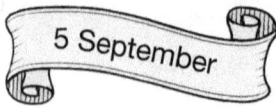

Pure and Simple

"If you can believe, all things are possible to him who believes." Immediately the father of the child cried out and
said with tears, "Lord, I believe; help my unbelief!"

~ Mark 9:23-24

When I was working through the book of 1 Timothy
in my quiet time, it struck me how concerned
Paul was about his young spiritual son Timothy.

Paul didn't want Timothy to pay any attention to any
foreign doctrine; rather he wanted him to keep to the
basics of Christianity, which is love from a pure heart,
a good conscience and a sincere faith (see 1 Tim. 1:5). I
firmly believe that Jesus is cautioning us today to keep
our faith pure and simple.

Unbelievers need help from God, and it is our duty to
lead them to Him. At the end of the day, it is the simple
message, the undiluted Word of God, that convicts
people to follow the Lord. It is the Gospel that draws
people to Him – not us. Keep it simple, keep it passionate,
keep it personal and keep it relevant. God will use you
powerfully.

Remember, if it is not in the Bible, do not listen to it.
Remember, you are not interested in people's opinion; it's only Gods opinion that counts! John 17:17
clearly says, "Sanctify them by Your truth. Your word is
truth."

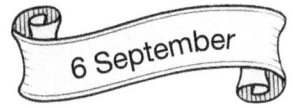

Live, Work and Talk

Therefore be imitators of God as dear children. And walk in love, as Christ also has loved us and given Himself for us, an offering and a sacrifice to God for a sweet-smelling aroma.

~ Ephesians 5:1-2

We are instructed very clearly in the Bible that we as believers are to walk and talk as followers of our Lord Jesus.

We need to speak life and encouragement to others, many of whom are down and depressed. We must remember that a kind word at the right time could, in fact, save someone's life. If we have nothing good to say then perhaps it is best to say nothing at all.

Encourage those who have been cast down. Talk life into those who are suffering from depression. Talk about peace to those who are in turmoil. Forgive those who have hurt you. Love the unloved. Get into the gutter with those who are lost and have given up hope. Restore them with the love of Christ. Feed His sheep.

You might not be a preacher or a church member. You might be a farmer, a housewife, a student, or un-employed, but that doesn't exempt you from feeding God's sheep. He wants you to feed His sheep. Feed them with what you say. Feed them with the love of Christ. Be Jesus to this dying world.

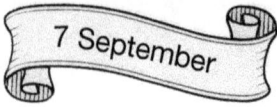

Jesus Is Love

And now abide faith, hope, love, these three; but the greatest of these is love.

~ 1 Corinthians 13:13

The most powerful force on earth is love! It is not hatred, or anger, or even fear, but love. And we, as Christians, spell love J-E-S-U-S.

In fact, 1 John 4:8 tells us that "he who does not love does not know God, for God is love." True love is a verb. It rolls up its sleeves. Yes, it goes beyond comfort and safety. It is more concerned about giving than receiving.

And what an example you and I have in our blessed Lord Jesus Christ. In John 15:13, Jesus said, "Greater love has no one than this, than to lay down one's life for his friends." The most powerful weapon we have as believers is love. When the love of Christ dominates you, overwhelms you and saturates you, people get saved. Love changes people's hearts – not hatred, fear, or intimidation.

To love is not a feeling, it is a decision. C. S. Lewis said, "Christian love, either towards God or towards man, is an affair of the will."

Let's make it our affair to love one another unconditionally, just like the Master said we should!

A Down Payment

... Who is the guarantee of our inheritance until the redemption of the purchased possession, to the praise of His glory.

~ Ephesians 1:14

In a world where there seems to be no guarantee of anything these days, people are desperately seeking for some sort of assurance.

But to those who belong to Christ, we have full assurance in Christ. He has promised to never leave us as orphans. He has sent us a "down payment," a guarantee that He is coming back very soon to take us to be with Him in paradise forever.

This guarantee that we have is His Holy Spirit, who has promised to never leave us nor forsake us (see Heb. 13:5). Allow the Holy Spirit to come into your life and change you. In the end, it is not so much what you say that will make a difference, but who you are.

As you go out today, allow the Spirit of God to lead you. If you put your trust in the Holy One of Israel today, you have nothing to fear. We walk by faith and not by sight.

As you focus your attention on the Holy Spirit that mountain you are facing at the moment will be transformed into a molehill. Trust in the Lord. He will never leave you.

Multitudes in the Valley of Decision

"The Spirit of the LORD is upon Me, because He has anointed Me to preach the gospel to the poor; He has sent Me to heal the brokenhearted, to proclaim liberty to the captives and recovery of sight to the blind, to set at liberty those who are oppressed."

~ Luke 4:18

A while back I preached to a crowd of people at Moreleta Park Church in Pretoria. About eight thousand people attended and we saw an unprecedented harvest of souls. Literally hundreds of people came forward to give their lives to Jesus Christ and publicly confessed Him as Lord of their lives.

There was much weeping, repentance and healing that took place as we felt the presence of Jesus moving and touching hearts. It is harvest time! Very rarely, in the forty years that I have been preaching, have I seen a harvest of first-time commitments like that.

There are many testimonies of God's miracle-working power and I'm as excited as ever about hearts turning back to the Lord. Please pray for this ministry as we are totally committed to revival. We need strength for the strain.

Let's make Mark 16:15 our driving force today: "Go into all the world and preach the gospel to every creature."

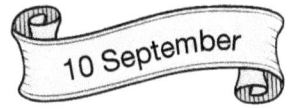

The Harvest

Put in the sickle, for the harvest is ripe. Come, go down; for the winepress is full, the vats overflow.

~ Joel 3:13

I've been farming for many years and one of the most dangerous things to do is to try and harvest a crop when it is not ripe – when it is still green and wet. When you put such a crop in the barn it goes mouldy and rots.

Another big no-no in farming is to leave the crop standing when it is time to harvest. This might be because the farmer is slack, lazy and does not have his reaping equipment in order. But once the crop lodges or falls over, like maize or wheat crops do, it is very difficult to lift it up again. When it rains, the crop rots in the field.

Timing is of the utmost importance at harvest time and the same rule applies when preaching the Gospel. Paul said in 1 Corinthians 9:16, "Woe is me if I do not preach the gospel." Because it is harvest time, all people need to have the opportunity to hear the gospel preached loud and clear. They need to know that they must be born again if they are seeking eternal life (see John 3:3).

Let's bring the crop in; it is white for harvest!

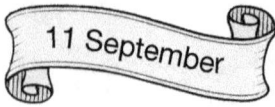

Get Back to Basics

"You must be born again."

~ John 3:7

I wrote the following many years ago in my Bible, "No time left! Got to speak up." That was written next to John 4:35 where Jesus says, "Do you not say, 'There are still four months and then comes the harvest'? Behold, I say to you, lift up your eyes and look at the fields, for they are already white for harvest."

The pastor once asked me before a service to please be very specific when making the altar call. He said often people come forward for numerous issues like bitterness, unforgiveness or fear. And then when the counsellors want to lead them in the prayer of salvation, they say that they are already believers. So, after the sermon, I made the call specifically for those who have never prayed the Sinner's Prayer before. I was astonished to see about 650 people come forward to be born again.

There was much weeping, brokenness and repentance, especially among the younger folk that day. They wanted the Gospel straight; the whole truth with none of the froth and bubbles. Let us roll up our sleeves and get to work. Let's get into the harvest fields, for the harvest is ripe and ready for reaping, but it must be the undiluted Gospel without all the frills.

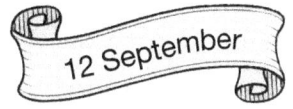

What Do You Expect?

Those who know Your name will put their trust in You;
for You, LORD, have not forsaken those who seek You.

~ Psalm 9:10

Have you recently asked yourself: In whom and what am I putting my trust and expectations? Is it based on your job, enterprise, relationships with friends and family, or even ministry?

Well, I want to sincerely warn you that if you put your hope and expectations in any one of these things you are going to be sorely disappointed!

King David put his hope and trust in many things and in many people. He was horribly let down. So he said in Psalm 62:5, "My soul, wait silently for God alone, for my expectation is from Him."

If you repent this morning and by faith you write down your expectations on a piece of paper, God will give you the desires of your heart. You see, if you spend time with God, then you will ask according to the will of God and He always answers such prayers.

God will make a way for you in a place where there seems to be no way. He will restore that which the rust and moth have tried to destroy, because He is God. Put your hope and trust in Jesus alone.

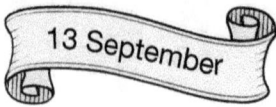

It's Time

"Do you not say, 'There are still four months and then comes the harvest'? Behold, I say to you, lift up your eyes and look at the fields, for they are already white for harvest!"

~ John 4:35

It's time to go out into the harvest fields! In the Gospel of Luke, specifically Luke 10:2, we read how Jesus sent out the seventy workers and gave them clear instruction to literally roll up their sleeves and get stuck in, because the harvest of lost souls is so very great!

The time is running out and there are multitudes of lost souls in the valley of decision. We have to press on with patience and perseverance, proclaiming the Gospel so that the Lord can gather the harvest when He returns. We have to be a letter of Christ that other people can read and turn their lives over to the Lord our God. It is not always easy to have the patience, endurance and perseverance to be a letter from Christ in this life.

Let's not waste any more time. In the classroom, the factory, sports field, the mines, on farms, in prisons and in hospitals – people are desperately waiting to hear the Good News. Jesus can help, forgive, restore and indeed, save them.

Therefore, my co-workers in Christ, let's get to work!

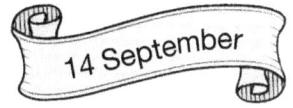

House Building

Unless the LORD builds the house, they labor in vain who build it; unless the LORD guards the city, the watchman stays awake in vain.

~ Psalm 127:1

God says clearly that if we don't build according to His blueprint, we will labour from early morning till late at night to no avail. We need to follow God's plans and invest in eternal things according to biblical principles. Then we will be blessed.

Matthew 6:33 says, "But seek first the kingdom of God and His righteousness, and all these things shall be added to you." Where do you stand today? Are you walking with God? Are you walking in His grace, or are you making your own plans?

We have exhausted all our own plans here in South Africa and they seem to have all failed. We as a nation need to unite regularly in prayer and ask God to build this beloved South Africa up for us.

Whatever venture you and I enter into, let us be quick to understand that unless God blesses it, we will not accomplish much. Seek the face of the Lord and find out what it is that He wants you to do.

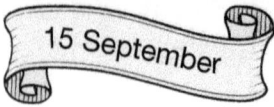

Godly Integrity

"God is not a man, that He should lie."

~ Numbers 23:19

When a barren woman nearly a hundred years old was told by God that she would fall pregnant and give birth to a son, she started laughing in disbelief. God asked her a question in Genesis 18:14, "Is anything too hard for the LORD?"

In Romans 4:20, the Bible says that Abraham remained strong in faith, giving glory to God. He was a hundred years old when God promised him that he'd be the father of all nations. In carnal eyes there was no hope for Abraham to have a family, let alone be the father of many nations.

Yet, because he had faith, God honoured him and Sarah. Sarah bore the most beautiful son, Isaac, and Abraham became the father of all believers today. As you take time to reflect on this miraculous story, you might also have some serious doubts in your own life caused by people who have disappointed you, broken their promises or lied to you.

Today, look to God alone for your dreams and your expectations, for He always makes good His promises to you, no matter what!

Trust in God's honesty and uprightness. If He said it, then He will surely do it, because it is not in His divine nature to be untrue to Himself.

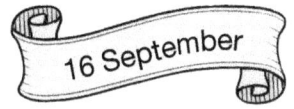

The Miraculous Catch

Some trust in chariots, and some in horses; but we will remember the name of the LORD our God.

~ Psalm 20:7

Crowds of people were no strangers to Jesus. And yet He is still the Lord of the individual! From the account in the Gospel of Luke, it's clear how Jesus stirred the hearts of people:

So it was, as the multitude pressed about Him to hear the word of God … He got into one of the boats, which was Simon's, and asked him to put out a little from the land. And He sat down and taught the multitudes from the boat. When He had stopped speaking, He said to Simon, "Launch out into the deep and let down your nets for a catch." But Simon answered and said to Him, "Master, we have toiled all night and caught nothing; nevertheless at Your word I will let down the net." And when they had done this, they caught a great number of fish … When Simon Peter saw it, he fell down at Jesus' knees, saying, "Depart from me, for I am a sinful man, O Lord!" For he and all who were with him were astonished at the catch of fish which they had taken (Luke 5:1-9).

Let us never forget that we serve a miracle-working God who is real, practical and more than able to take care of our every need in this life, both physically and spiritually. Indeed, I have seen it happen in my own life.

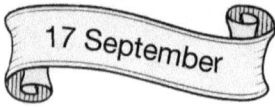

I Will Be Your God

"You shall be My people, and I will be your God."

~ Jeremiah 30:22

What an incredibly comforting promise, especially in the troubled times in which we are living. Yet the Lord requires from us two things: faithfulness and obedience. He is a jealous God and will not tolerate the worshipping of any other gods before Him. If we put Him above all else, then He shall be a friend to us.

Romans 8:31 tells us clearly that "if God is for us, who can be against us?" Hallelujah! We are in the majority because Jesus Christ is for us.

One thing the Lord does not tolerate is when you try to serve two masters, becoming unfaithful to Him and standing with one foot in the world and one foot in the Kingdom. Either you are for Him, or you are against Him (see Matt. 12:30). He is definitely for you.

We need to nail our colours to the mast and give Him first priority in our lives. We need to honour Him because He is a good God; not for what you can get out of Him, but just because He is who He is.

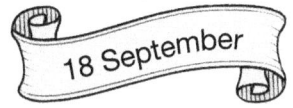

The Power of Prayer

"Watch and pray, lest you enter into temptation. The spirit indeed is willing, but the flesh is weak."

~ Mark 14:38

Jesus calls us to watch and pray, lest we fall into temptation. Why?

Because when we walk by sight (in the flesh), we cannot see a way out for our beloved South Africa. However, when we pray the prayer of faith according to God's Word, we can see the Red Sea parting before our very spiritual eyes. Then we will observe a supernatural turnaround in our nation (see Exod. 14:13-14).

The future of our nation, indeed the future of the world, does not depend on anyone else, but solely upon the Christian. As we go out to work today, let us remember that people are hanging onto every word we say, listening to everything that comes out of our mouths and watching everything we do. They will receive your message as if it were coming from God because you are representing Him – even if the message is negative.

Let us walk, talk and follow the example of Jesus Christ. Let us trust Jesus our Saviour with raw, undiluted faith for the ultimate peace and prosperity of our beloved South Africa.

Do It God's Way

Blessed is the man who walks not in the counsel of the ungodly, but his delight is in the law of the LORD. He shall be like a tree planted by the rivers of water.

~ Psalm 1:1-3

There is no such thing as a coincidence in the Kingdom of God; everything is a God-incidence. It is no coincidence that God's children do well in life. They obey God's principles and live according to His Heavenly mandate. Because of this they succeed. This is not luck, for we as believers do not believe in luck.

We trust in God's abundant blessing on our lives, which comes by obeying His instructions daily (see Prov. 3:5-6). Jesus alone is the Director of our paths.

It's not by coincidence that God blesses His obedient children. He is able to do so because they listen to Him and obey His instructions. You can either believe that the Lord answers prayer, or you can say it is a coincidence. However, as a Christian, you cannot continue to think it is coincidence for the rest of your life. We serve a mighty God who expects us to pursue and to persist in prayer. If you keep knocking on that door, it's going to open. God honours the fervent prayer of the righteous.

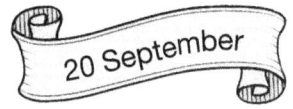

Close to the Kingdom

Now when Jesus saw that he answered wisely, He said to him, "You are not far from the kingdom of God."

~ Mark 12:34

Jesus came to earth to fulfil what is written in the Bible. When the scribe asked Jesus, "Which is the greatest commandment of all?" our Lord promptly answered by quoting straight from Deuteronomy 6:4-5, which reads: "Love the LORD your God with all your heart, with all your soul, and with all your strength."

Then Jesus added to the Greatest Commandment of all, the second, which is to love our neighbour as ourselves (see Lev. 19:18)! This act is better than offering sacrifices and burnt offerings.

The Lord is not interested in your ability; He wants your availability. Don't worry about standing up and performing great acts or speeches. Rather, let us be doers of the Word in small ways, so people can come to us for a cup of tea or a warm meal, as well as for spiritual nourishment and encouragement. Start in your own home and with those closest to you. That is what Jesus did: He ministered to His friends and family.

God first gives you your vision then you slowly build on that layer by layer. Start praying and serving where you are; take what you've got and use it to serve the nearest person to you.

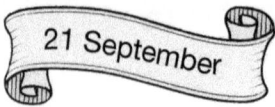

An Undivided Heart

"You shall receive power when the Holy Spirit has come upon you; and you shall be witnesses to Me in Jerusalem, and in all Judea and Samaria, and to the end of the earth."

~ Acts 1:8

The disciples needed the power of the Holy Spirit and zeal to proclaim the Gospel. Charles Spurgeon said, "Like a chariot without horses, like the sun without heat and a Heaven without joy, is a man of God without zeal."

If there is no fire, there is no sacrifice. We can prepare our offering; we can place the stones in place; we can cut the firewood and stack it correctly; we can kill the ox and put it on the altar … but without fire there can be no burnt offering. We cannot have zeal if we do not know Him.

I have heard many sermons preached that have obviously been prepared for weeks in advance. The speaker has got every single Scripture matched up with every single illustration, but it is dead and boring. Why? Because the fire of the Holy Spirit was not present.

When we tell people about Jesus, we need to speak from our heart. Charles Finney, one of the greatest evangelists of all time, said, "There can be no revival when Mr. Amen and Mr. Wet-Eyes are not found in the audience."

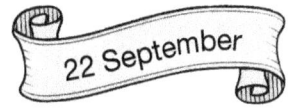

The Upside-Down Gospel

"Whoever receives one of these little children in My name receives Me; and whoever receives Me, receives not Me but Him who sent Me."

~ Mark 9:37

The mighty Baobab tree is also called the upside-down tree, because when it loses its leaves in winter, its branches look like roots sticking up in the air.

The Gospel of Jesus Christ is the same – if we want to be the greatest in the Kingdom of God, then we must be prepared to be the least and the servant of all (see Mark 9:35).

I have the most beautiful little granddaughter, her name is Rebecca. When I spend time with her, it is so refreshing to see her innocence, her trust in me and her absolute joy in the little things of life – yes, her sheer childlikeness.

Jesus says we need to become more childlike if we are to see the Kingdom of God. We need to trust Him more, believe Him more and most of all to love Him more with childlike faith! Then we will start to see things change for the better in our lives.

We need to serve our brothers and sisters as humble servants while we still have time. You see, the word "minister" actually means "to serve." Humility is a sign of a great child of God.

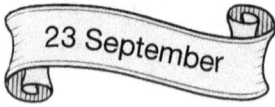

Do Not Be Afraid

They all saw Him and were troubled. But immediately He talked with them and said to them, "Be of good cheer! It is I; do not be afraid."

~ Mark 6:50

What kind of storm are you facing in your life today? Well, our miracle-working God, who is the same yesterday, today and forever, is saying to you and me, "Do not be afraid." He can calm the storm in your life with one word.

Just look at what He'd done for the disciples. They thought the boat was about to sink and that they were all going to drown:

"Jesus was sleeping at the back of the boat. The disciples woke Him up, shouting, 'Teacher, don't You care that we're going to drown?' When Jesus woke up, He rebuked the wind and said to the waves, 'Silence! Be still!' Suddenly the wind stopped, and there was a great calm. Then He asked them, 'Why are you afraid? Do you still have no faith?'" (Mark 4:38-40 NLT).

We all experience storms in this life. Some storms pass quickly while other storms sweep us off our feet and fill us with fear and grief. What do we do then? We turn to Jesus Christ. He can take care of any problem and any need we might have. When we put our trust in Him, He will calm the storm and fill us with His peace.

Something to Eat

> But He answered and said to them, "You give them something to eat." And they said to Him, "Shall we go and buy two hundred denarii worth of bread and give them something to eat?"
>
> ~ Mark 6:37

Jesus told His disciples when they were staring at 5 000 hungry men, not counting the women and children, "You feed them."

The first thing the disciples did was to try and make a plan to feed the multitudes, saying that they had counted up all their money and had a few denarii (see Mark 6:37) – a hopeless situation.

That's where faith and obedience come in. A boy offered his lunch of two fish and five barley loaves of bread. Then something amazing happened:

> [Jesus] commanded the multitudes to sit down. And He took the five loaves and the two fish, and looking up to heaven, He blessed and broke and gave the loaves to the disciples; and the disciples gave to the multitudes. So they all ate and were filled (Matt. 14:19-20).

Jesus is asking us a question today: What do you have in your hand? If you have something to offer, give it to Him and He will feed the masses. He will conquer the giants in your life!

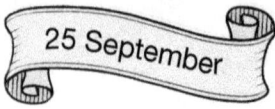

Footprints in the Sand

You do not know what will happen tomorrow. For what is your life? It is even a vapor that appears for a little time and then vanishes away.

~ James 4:14

In a little seaside village there is a sign next to the beach that says, "When you leave, let only your footprints remain."

Some time ago, I was informed that one of my childhood friends had sadly passed away. I sat quietly by myself for a moment and reflected on my childhood years in Zambia, where we went to school together. In the afternoons, after we had our lunch and finished our homework, we'd cycle down to the municipal swimming pool and played together. Just about every weekend, we would stay over at each other's houses. We literally grew up together.

Our friendship started more than sixty years ago and yet I can remember it as if it were yesterday.

James 4 says that our lives are but a vapour, here today and gone tomorrow. We do not have time to waste arguing, holding grudges, or fighting over trivial matters. Life is too short for that!

You see, what the little signboard on the beach didn't say was that when the tide comes in, it will wash away your footprints. The only thing that remains is memories. Make sure that they're good ones.

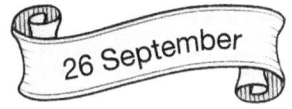

A Doorkeeper for the King

For a day in Your courts is better than a thousand. I would rather be a doorkeeper in the house of my God than dwell in the tents of wickedness.

~ Psalm 84:10

I have to agree wholeheartedly with the psalmist – to be a doorkeeper in the house of the Lord even for one day, is far better than to spend a thousand days elsewhere! And the older I get, the more I realise that the world truly holds nothing of any real value to me.

You know the saying, "Been there, done that, got the T-shirt." I have a few of them, but they really don't mean much to me at all. Yet to have an encounter with the living God is something out of this world.

Mother Teresa didn't have much in this world, but then again, she had everything. She had a purpose for living; she had a divine vision. She had Jesus Christ in her life. That's why her circumstances did not affect her negatively. That's why she could live the vision and calling she received from God.

I love the words from Fanny J. Crosby's hymn that says, "Take the world, but give me Jesus." This is so true for me and I pray for you too.

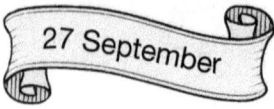

The Written Word

"Write the vision and make it plain."

~ Habakkuk 2:2

Reader Harris, who was a prominent barrister and mentor of the well-known evangelist Oswald Chambers, once said, "Probably the most lasting of all preaching is with the pen."

The Holy Spirit strongly impressed upon me again to keep writing. All of us have a story to tell about how Jesus has influenced our lives in one way or another.

For me, and it still warms my heart to this day, it was coming back from mission trips, passing through the rural villages in Africa and seeing the local people sitting under shady trees, absorbed in reading the Bibles we had distributed to them.

C. T. Studd (1860-1931) was a great English cricketer. He went out into the mission field and spread the Gospel with all of his heart. He gave up everything he had, gave away his fortune and died in the Congo, preaching the Gospel. He said, "The suspicions subtract. Faith adds. But love multiplies. It blesses twice – him who gives it and him who gets it."

We are in this world, but we are not of this world. We are here to fulfil our calling – to spread the Gospel of Jesus Christ and lead people to faith in Him. Are you living your calling today?

Immanuel – God with Us

When You did awesome things for which we did not look, You came down, the mountains shook at Your presence. For since the beginning of the world men have not heard nor perceived by the ear, nor has the eye seen any God besides You, who acts for the one who waits for Him.

~ Isaiah 64:3-4

I am so grateful to the Lord Jesus for coming down from Heaven to earth; for walking the road before us and for showing us the way.

I thank the Lord for revealing Himself to us in so many miraculous ways. So much so that no one could ever possibly hope to persuade me that He is not God made flesh, our Immanuel. He has personally shown me how He can change the weather. Not once, but many times when I have earnestly and desperately prayed the prayer of faith.

First Corinthians 2:9 (NLT) says, "No eye has seen, no ear has heard, and no mind has imagined what God has prepared for those who love Him."

Though our loved ones may not be with us, God is "with us" through His Holy Spirit in us. As His children, may we share His love with special tenderness and sensitivity, celebrating the healing God who never leaves us.

May God bless you as you also walk the path of faith.

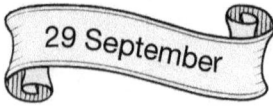

Sign and Wonders

You are of God, little children, and have overcome them, because He who is in you is greater than he who is in the world.

~ 1 John 4:4

One genuine miracle equals a thousand sermons. It was not through Jesus' preaching that the people recognised Him as the Son of God, but through the signs, wonders and miracles that He performed wherever He went.

In Mark 1:23-28, Jesus casted out an unclean spirit. The people were amazed and asked, "What is this? What new doctrine is this?" They were astounded by the authority Jesus used to cast out the evil spirit.

His fame quickly spread throughout the whole region of Galilee. I urge you today to pray for the sick, to believe in miracles and not to be afraid of the evil one.

The most powerful thing about a miracle is that nobody can dispute it. The man who once was blind is now able to see; he who was lame can now walk. People must work out for themselves who did it. All we know is that there's only one power that operates on this earth and that is the power of the Holy Spirit manifested through the sons and daughters of God.

Do Not Procrastinate

"For what will it profit a man if he gains the whole world, and loses his own soul?"

~ Mark 8:36

While we are still alive, we need to continue to work on our relationships with one another. Remember the saying, "Charity begins at home"? There is no point in trying to tell people all the way on the other side of the world about the love of God when we cannot get it right at home.

We need to make the most of the time we have left here on earth and not grow old with regrets, wishing we could have told people while they were still alive. We need to build bridges. Don't get distracted or sidetracked. Remain focused.

We need to settle any quarrels that we have between each other. There is nothing worse than to say, "I wish I had told my father that I loved him before he died." Rather tell him while he is still alive.

Let's get our priorities in order. Let's be men and women who are walking according to the plan laid out by the Lord Jesus Christ. While we are still alive, let us put right anything in our hearts holding us back and move forward in faith.

October

May God give you more and more grace and peace.
~ 2 Peter 1:2 NLT ~

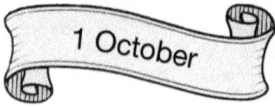

Walk by Faith

For we walk by faith, not by sight.

~ 2 Corinthians 5:7

God always honours faith. I have experienced this so many times in my own life. God gives me a clear word and then He will confirm it to me. By faith, I need to walk out of fear, out of doubt, out of discouragement and into the realm of faith.

In these last days before the coming of the Lord, more faith is going to be required from us as believers. I want to encourage you to exercise your faith. Start to believe God for small things, and God will honour His word like He always does. That will increase your faith to believe for bigger things.

Back in 2003, when the Lord asked me through His Word to mentor some young men, by faith I agreed. I had no idea what was going to happen. The result was the Mighty Men conferences that are still well-attended and reaching thousands of men around the world every year.

Faith begets faith, and faith is contagious. We must walk by faith and remain faithful to God. We never know what great plans God has in store for us.

A Light to Guide Me

Your word is a lamp to my feet and a light to my path.
~ Psalm 119:105

How do you get to your destination? You do it one step at a time and by putting one foot in front of the other. Many of us do not know the way, but we know God, and He will direct our path. That is how we are going to complete our long journey here on earth: one step at a time.

Many young people want to know: "What is my destination; where is the end of my journey?" We don't know precisely, and we don't *have* to know; all we have to do is know the One who is leading us. If we continue doing right and living according to God's principles, He will make a way for us. The Lord says in Revelation 3:8, "I know your works. See, I have set before you an open door, and no one can shut it; for you have a little strength, have kept My word, and have not denied My name."

If we live according to God's mandate for our lives, we will eventually arrive safely and in good time at our destination. Just keep putting one foot in front of the other and you will be sure not to only reach your destination, but to see your faith become a reality.

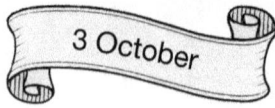

Keep Your Eyes on Jesus

"For the LORD God will help Me; therefore I will not be disgraced; therefore I have set My face like a flint, and I know that I will not be ashamed."

~ Isaiah 50:7

I have never once been disgraced or ashamed when I have put my trust in God. The Lord has promised us that He will help us. When a task seems too big for you, take your eyes off the task and look at the Lord; the task will literally disappear.

God is as big as we allow Him to be in our lives. When I was in Sweden preaching at a church, a woman started weeping. She said to me, "We have everything we need here but we keep Jesus in a matchbox and every now and again we let Him out." That saddened my heart so much.

If you give the Lord everything you've got – and it might only be two fishes and five barley loaves – He will take it by faith and He will multiply it for you.

The Lord will help those who put their trust in Him, and He will never allow them to be disgraced. Let us keep our eyes on Jesus. If we do that, we will finish the task He has set before us, and we will rise above our challenges.

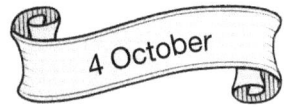

Forgive One Another

Make allowance for each other's faults, and forgive anyone who offends you. Remember, the Lord forgave you, so you must forgive others.

~ Colossians 3:13 NLT

The Lord says we are to forgive one another, bear with one another and tolerate one another, because God has done the same for us. As the Lord forgives us for all our sins, we need to forgive one another.

Pray for the people who have hurt you. You need to pray for them so that they will forgive you, as you have forgiven them.

If you are honest with yourself, you might admit that there are some people who are not even aware that they have done anything to you. They are carrying on with their lives, blissfully unaware of the hurt or bitterness they caused, and it is holding you back. Ask God to take that unforgiveness out of your heart. Then forgive that person and move on with your life.

We need to forgive one another, and then we need to move along. The Bible tells us that when God forgives, He forgets (see Heb. 8:12 and Jer. 31:34). God never holds a grudge. You will find that even as you forgive that person who hurt you, a tremendous burden will fall off your shoulders and you will be free.

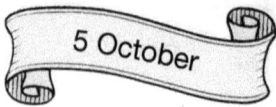

Find Your Vision

Where there is no vision, the people perish ...

~ Proverbs 29:18 KJV

After I gave my life to Jesus Christ, He gave me a vision, a blueprint to follow and a new hope. If you have no vision, ask the Lord sincerely to give you one and He will. He will give you a short-term vision and a long-term vision.

In Habakkuk 2:2-3, the Lord says, "Write the vision, and make it plain on tablets, that he may run who reads it. For the vision is yet for an appointed time; but at the end it will speak, and it will not lie. Though it tarries, wait for it; because it will surely come, it will not tarry."

Ask the Lord to give you a vision and it will come. It might be for a season ahead, but it will happen. There are things that I can do well, which God has gifted me to do, and things I am not so good at.

We are all like that. We all have different gifts, every single one of us. Someone might have a wonderful musical talent, or be a great builder, or be a good preacher, or might be skilled at taking care of the poor and the needy. Whatever your vision and purpose is, stick to it and God will use it for His Kingdom.

Make Today Count

See then that you walk circumspectly, not as fools but as wise, redeeming the time, because the days are evil.

~ Ephesians 5:15-16

We live only a very short time here on earth. I was riding my mountain bike early one morning and came across some beautiful yellow flowers, but I knew they probably would be gone by the next day.

Today is the only day that we have. Let's do what the Lord tells us to do. Do not become a procrastinator and say, "I'll do it tomorrow" because it will never happen. Never leave off for tomorrow what you can do today.

I know a man who is so passionate about the Lord that when I gave my life to Jesus he encouraged me to hold campaigns. To my knowledge he has not organised one event himself. Every time I used to speak to him, he would say, "As soon as I get my pension, I'll start." Then later it was, "As soon as I get my business going, I will start," and so it went on.

Remember, we have only today; we cannot bank on tomorrow. We really need to redeem this moment that we have. Get out there and get started, and Jesus Christ will do the rest.

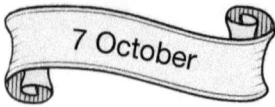

Stay the Course

You, who once were alienated and enemies in your mind by wicked works, yet now He has reconciled in the body of His flesh through death, to present you holy, and blameless, and above reproach in His sight.

~ Colossians 1:21-22

We can never walk away from the gift the Lord Jesus Christ has given to us, which is eternal life. Faithfulness to the end is essential in the Christian life. You can't start well and finish poorly, and expect to go to Heaven. It doesn't work like that. When we build our house, we build it on solid rock and not on shifting sand. The Lord says in Matthew 10:22, "You will be hated by all for My name's sake. But he who endures to the end will be saved."

We've got to keep focused and we've got to keep moving forward. Doubt is one of the things that can rob us of our confidence in the Lord, and we know that doubt and unbelief often go hand in hand.

Do not allow yourself to drift away into doubt and unbelief, but rather stand firm in your faith. Rest assured and believe with all of your heart, soul, mind and strength that Jesus Christ saves. For that we need to be eternally thankful.

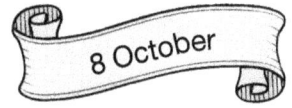

The Father's House

"In My Father's house are many mansions; if it were not so, I would have told you. I go to prepare a place for you. And if I go and prepare a place for you, I will come again and receive you to Myself; that where I am, there you may be also."

~ John 14:2-3

The preparation of the bridegroom is different to the preparation of the bride. The bridegroom goes and prepares a place for his bride to live. Accordingly, Jesus has gone ahead to prepare a place for us where we will live forever with Him.

We need to live according to God's Holy Word, and prepare ourselves physically, mentally and spiritually for the great wedding day.

Somebody asked me if we will see our loved ones in Heaven. I can firmly say, "Definitely for those who have been born again, we will definitely see them in Heaven!" That is why the Lord Jesus has gone ahead to prepare a place for us.

Our God is holy and we will only be with Him when we believe and acknowledge Him as Lord and Saviour. Romans 10:9 confirms, "If you confess with your mouth the Lord Jesus and believe in your heart that God has raised Him from the dead, you will be saved."

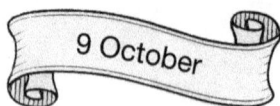

Come Aside

The report went around concerning Him all the more; and great multitudes came together to hear, and to be healed by Him of their infirmities. So He Himself often withdrew into the wilderness and prayed.

~ Luke 5:15-16

When we get busy, we spend less time with God; but when Jesus got busier, He spent more time with His Father and more time withdrawing from the public. Prayer is the lifeline between people and God. The evangelist Smith Wigglesworth said, "I never pray for more than thirty minutes; but I never let thirty minutes go by without praying." For him prayer was a lifestyle.

It was the same with our Lord Jesus Christ: He regularly withdrew to be on His own with His Father. Why was this? It was because it was the only way He could complete the mammoth task that He had. He needed to continually receive spiritual and physical strength from His Father.

We cannot just keep on keeping on; even as I write this, I am very conscious of that. All work and no time spent with God is physically and spiritually draining and we have nothing left to offer. Let us always prioritise prayer time with our Lord.

A Healthy Fear of the Lord

"Behold, the fear of the LORD, that is wisdom, and to depart from evil is understanding."

~ Job 28:28

Happy is the person who has a fear of doing wrong – someone who is afraid of committing sin lest they offend their loving God. It is much better to avoid sin than to carelessly fall into it, and then to be totally destroyed.

Psalm 119:1 (NIV) says, "Blessed are those whose ways are blameless, who walk according to the law of the LORD." If we are going to respect God and His principles, and live our lives according to His Holy Word, then we will live peaceful and fulfilled lives. To fear God means to have a reverence for Him, to respect Him and to obey Him. These are the things that will keep us from falling into sinful ways.

One of the most dangerous things to do as a Christian is to compromise. Once we compromise our faith, then we are on a downward spiral, which picks up momentum until we are far from God. It is impossible to maintain a prayer relationship with Jesus while knowingly breaking His law.

Matthew 12:30 declares, "He who is not with Me is against Me, and he who does not gather with Me scatters abroad."

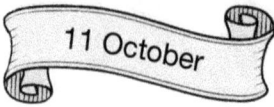

The Power of the Bible

"So shall My word be that goes forth from My mouth; it shall not return to Me void, but it shall accomplish what I please, and it shall prosper in the thing for which I sent it."

~ Isaiah 55:11

I have been asked by many people about how I hear from God. It is quite simple actually: it first requires discipline to rise early in the morning, and it requires diligent study of God's Word. It requires spending time reading the Bible every single day.

This should be done systematically: read a portion in the Old Testament and in the New Testament. Soon the Word of God will start to speak to your heart and confirm things that you need answers for. Apply the word that God has given to you, and you will see that the Lord confirms it with practical, physical evidence.

As a young man when I was farming, I would wait on the Lord at the beginning of the season to seek direction with regard to the crops I should plant, what number and when I should plant. Every season God would show me through His Word.

Then I would apply it and by faith believe God for the outcome, and not once has the Lord ever failed me. This is the awesome God we serve!

Rolling the Dice

Though He slay me, yet will I trust Him.

~ Job 13:15

There are no coincidences in God's world. If you look back on your own life, you'll see that everything has been allowed and done for a purpose. At the time, some of the things that happened to you seemed absolutely hopeless. But the Lord has never forsaken us, and He has never left us.

Now as a Christian, I must confess that there is no more "hoping for the best" – it is prayer, and then doing exactly what God tells us to do through His Word. We thank the Lord for His loving-kindness and we know that no matter what happens, He will use it for good.

I know many people who will not walk under a ladder, because they say it's bad luck. They won't cross two knives at a dining table, believing it is bad luck. So it goes on and on. But I know there are no coincidences in God's planning; everything works out for a reason and God is in full control of everything.

We must remember that we do live in a fallen world, and because of that, things do not always go the way we would hope them to go. But even in tragedy, God can triumph and turn evil into good (see Rom. 8:28).

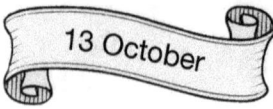

The Only Road

Jesus said to him, "I am the way, the truth, and the life. No one comes to the Father except through Me."

~ John 14:6

Many of us think that there are different ways in which we can achieve eternal life. That is a fallacy, totally untrue. Jesus says very clearly that He is the only way; there is no other way to Heaven but through Him. There is no other road that leads to eternal life.

There are many countries in the world where, if you were to stand up in public and unashamedly tell people that Jesus Christ is the only way to Heaven, you would be arrested and thrown in jail, or even worse – killed. However, it is the truth. When people mention the name of the Saviour of the world, Jesus Christ, it seems as if everyone is offended and whoever spoke His holy name must apologise for their faith.

The devil hates the name of Jesus Christ, because he knows that is the name that leads the multitudes home. We have an obligation, as followers of Jesus, to direct the lost along the true way that leads to eternal life.

When a person asks you about salvation or Heaven, you need to point them to Jesus Christ, and to Him alone.

Walking on Water

Wait on the LORD; be of good courage, and He shall strengthen your heart; wait, I say, on the LORD!

~ Psalm 27:14

Psalm 46:10 says, "Be still, and know that I am God." One of the absolute hardest things to do as a Christian in these turbulent times is to wait. He is truly worth waiting for, but the secret is that while we are waiting, we need to keep positive, keep our spirits up and expect answers to our prayers.

It is the heart that needs calming and positive joy. Our God has all the power and all the strength we need. He can change your life entirely if you are brave enough to be patient, to wait on God.

While organising a prayer meeting, I said to people that I felt that I was walking on the water, and the further out I got the bigger the waves were becoming. There was no turning back. All I could see was the light in front of me, and that is Jesus Christ.

I dare not look to the left, or to the right, because I would surely sink, just like Peter did when Jesus asked him to walk to Him on the water. But I know that if I keep my eyes on Him, I will safely reach the shore.

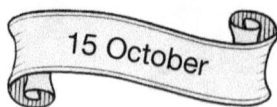

Faith as a Mustard Seed

"If you have faith as a mustard seed, you will say to this mountain, 'Move from here to there,' and it will move; and nothing will be impossible for you."

~ Matthew 17:20

Saint Augustine said, "Faith is to believe what you do not yet see; the reward for this faith is to see what you believed."

I realise that we do nothing; the Lord does it all, but we've got to trust Him. If we do things God's way, He gets all the glory. That's happened in my life numerous times, when God has come through for me in such a magnificent way that I could never touch His glory. People could see it was a work of God from a mile away.

I carry little bottles of mustard seed around in my pocket and, when I'm travelling, I often feel led to give a few of them away. Often, the person will become tearful and say, "I really needed to remember that today." I tell the person to keep that little bottle of mustard seeds in their pocket.

When you hold a bottle of mustard seeds in your hand, your focus is removed from the mountain to God. It is a reminder that with faith the size of a mustard seed, Jesus will give you the strength to overcome your mountain.

Keep the Faith

They must be committed to the mystery of the faith now revealed and must live with a clear conscience.

~ 1 Timothy 3:9 NLT

We need to persist in prayer, not looking for one big solution, but slowly, inch by inch, pray for the salvation, safety and security of our loved ones in the name of Jesus Christ. Before the rain comes there are dark clouds, until eventually there is a cloudburst and life-giving rain falls. Never stop praying, loving and believing for the salvation of your loved one.

If there is one thing farming has taught me, it is persistence. When you plant a crop, whether it is potatoes, maize, cabbages or tomatoes, it is not a once-off thing. It is a step by step, little by little, day by day exercise, until you reap a bountiful harvest.

I think of George Müller, a man of great faith who started an orphanage, later known as the Müller Homes in Bristol. Here he cared for 10,000 children during his lifetime. He established 117 schools that have offered 120,000 children a Christian education.

After he was saved, his life was turned around in an instant. He became one of the greatest ambassadors for Jesus Christ that this world has seen. People need the Lord and the way they find Him is through the faithful prayers and persistence of God's children.

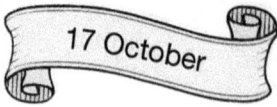

Safely under His Wings

Surely He shall deliver you from the snare of the fowler and from the perilous pestilence. He shall cover you with His feathers, and under His wings you shall take refuge.

~ Psalm 91:3-4

A pastor in Port Elizabeth told me that he was once walking in the Drakensberg Mountains. There was a bushfire sometime before his stroll and as he was walking along, he saw the charred remains of a quail. She was lying with her wings spread out, and the bushfire had caught her, ran right over her and burnt all her feathers.

He picked up the remains of the charred bird, only to find underneath her a brood of little chicks that the mother had protected from the fire, perfectly safe.

This reminds me of Luke 13:34, where Jesus says, "How often I wanted to gather your children together, as a hen gathers her brood under her wings, but you were not willing!" We need to allow the Lord Jesus Christ to take us under His wings and protect us. Jesus loves His people with a love we will never fully understand on earth.

Let us today allow the Prince of glory to protect us. Let us put our trust in Him, because He will not allow us to be burnt by the fires and hardship of this earthly life.

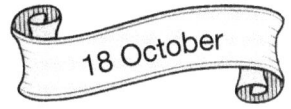

Pick Your Thoughts

Whatever things are true, whatever things are noble, whatever things are just, whatever things are pure, whatever things are lovely, whatever things are of good report, if there is any virtue and if there is anything praiseworthy – meditate on these things.

~ Philippians 4:8

We need to be very careful where we concentrate our thoughts. If we focus on evil things, they will fester and grow inside of us and eventually lead us to sin. We have to really concentrate on the things of God and not allow the pressures and the fears of this world to dominate our thoughts.

This robs us of our joy and, even more importantly, of our faith in God. When that happens, we become sitting ducks for the evil one to take us out.

Psalm 8:4 asks, "What is man that You are mindful of him, and the son of man that You visit him?" God loves us so much, and all He wants us to do is to spend time with Him. That is why spending time with God each day is absolutely vital.

We need to take our thoughts captive (see 2 Cor. 10:5), give them to Jesus and let Him develop them into positive, constructive thoughts that will make you the man or woman of God that you were meant to be.

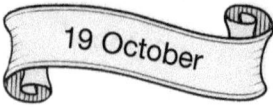

Forsaken and Shamed for Us

"Most assuredly, I say to you, he who hears My word and believes in Him who sent Me has everlasting life, and shall not come into judgment, but has passed from death into life."

~ John 5:24

The cross represents pain, suffering and humiliation. The Cross is a constant reminder to the believer of what Jesus Christ did for us. We know that the cross is empty, praise be to God. He is not even in the tomb; the tomb is empty.

The Saviour of the world is seated comfortably at the right hand of our Heavenly Father, and He is preparing to come back a second time. But when He comes, He will not be coming back as the Saviour of the world riding on a donkey, but He will come as the Commander of the armies of Heaven riding a white horse (see Rev. 19:11, 14). He will be coming as the Supreme Judge.

Jesus relinquished all His power, dignity and royalty and allowed Himself to be exposed and shamed, so that we might be saved from eternal damnation. We have a tremendous responsibility to tell people the wonderful good news that there is a better way – there is a Saviour who loves them, One who can wash away all their sins and give them new life.

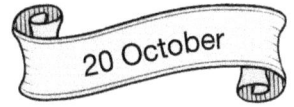

Keep It Simple

Christ did not send me to baptize, but to preach the gospel, not with wisdom of words, lest the cross of Christ should be made of no effect.

~ 1 Corinthians 1:17

The Lord wants us to keep our relationship with Him simple – there is no need to complicate the Word of God. The parables that Jesus told are so simple that young children can even understand them perfectly. I have many grandchildren and they all enjoy the parables. We need to keep our faith simple.

John Maxwell wrote, "Educators take something simple and make it complicated. Communicators take something complicated and make it simple." People don't want long explanations of Scripture. People want the Gospel, but they want it straight and they want it simple. We mustn't unnecessarily read too much into things. First Corinthians 1:19 (NLT) says, "I will destroy the wisdom of the wise and discard the intelligence of the intelligent."

I have no problem with learning or with those who have gone to a Bible college and studied theology. In fact, I envy those scholars, because I love the Word of God so very much. However, the average man in the street wants the Gospel of Jesus Christ in its simplicity and in its untainted, life-transforming way. Let us always be mindful of sharing our faith in a simple and uncomplicated way.

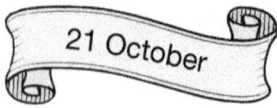

A Protective God

"I, the LORD your God, am a jealous God, visiting the iniquity of the fathers upon the children to the third and fourth generations of those who hate Me, but showing mercy to thousands, to those who love Me and keep My commandments."

~ Exodus 20:5-6

The word *jealous* has a double meaning. For instance, I am very "jealous" of my wife because I love her so much, and I do not want other people manhandling her or treating her badly. In a similar way, the Lord God loves us very much and He does not want us making carved images or serving other gods. He is jealous of our love for Him.

Anything you put before God in your life becomes an idol, and that is what makes the Lord very upset. We need to make time to be with Him, to have fellowship with Him, to obey His commandments and to walk in His ways. However, His relationship with us is not a possessive relationship. I am talking about a jealousy that is pure, where God loves us so extravagantly that He becomes fiercely protective of His people.

It saddens God's heart when we turn our backs on Him and chase after the things of this world. He paid a tremendous price for our salvation and He wants us to prosper and He wants us to be successful. Make Him the most important thing in your life.

Sons and Daughters of the King

"A hireling, he who is not the shepherd, one who does not own the sheep, sees the wolf coming and leaves the sheep and flees; and the wolf catches the sheep and scatters them. The hireling flees because he is a hireling and does not care about the sheep."

~ John 10:12-13

There is a huge difference between a hireling and your own child. On our farm we have honest and hardworking employees. They genuinely have the interests of our farm at heart, but they work for a salary. They do not work for an inheritance.

This farm belongs to my children and they are not working for a salary or a wage; they are working for their birthright. This makes them work harder because they are working for themselves and their own future. Conversely, the hireling will knock off at 5 o'clock.

Jesus died for you and me. We are His sons and daughters. We are going to inherit eternal life; therefore, we need to act like sons and daughters. We must hang in there even when the job gets tough.

God's children do not turn their back on Him, because they are not living for this life but for eternity. Sons and daughters are living for their reward in Heaven, knowing that the best is yet to come.

Find Your Sabbath Day

"Hypocrite! Does not each one of you on the Sabbath loose his ox or donkey from the stall, and lead it away to water it?"
~ Luke 13:15

In Luke 13, after Jesus had healed a woman, the Pharisees rebuked Jesus for working on the Sabbath. We know that the Lord created the Sabbath for His people, not His people for the Sabbath. He wants us to work for six days and rest on the seventh day.

Jesus could see straight through the hypocrisy of the Pharisees. The people weren't really concerned about the Sabbath; they just wanted to catch out the Son of God so they could kill Him.

One of the things that keeps people out of church is when they see hypocrisy taking place inside the church. On Sunday morning, everybody's nicely dress-ed, hands raised, praising the Lord, and then on Monday they go back to living as non-believers. The Lord has no time for such behaviour, and it is a very poor witness for Jesus Christ.

We need to prioritise our time with the Lord on the Sabbath as well as with our loved ones. We need a day each week to rest, to pray and to worship the Lord, and to spend time with each other and build each other up in the things of God.

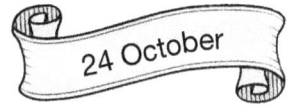

The Rest the Lord Gives

"My Presence will go with you, and I will give you rest."
~ Exodus 33:14

Every morning, I have a quiet time before I start work. That time is absolutely crucial for me – if I don't have that prayer time, I am restless the whole day.

I find myself prioritising work that is not important and neglecting the work I should be doing. I'm not thinking straight because I have not been resting in the Lord. Matthew 11:28 says, "Come to Me, all you who labor and are heavy laden, and I will give you rest."

I have heard of many men who have worked their whole lives, reaching the top of their field as GMs, CEOs and directors of large organisations. They can't wait to retire to their beach cottage, fish to their heart's content and enjoy life.

Often I later hear that these individuals passed away within two or three years because they had nothing to do – they had lost their vision and no longer had a purpose. When we rest in the Lord, we have peace within our souls.

We cannot have peace in our hearts without the presence of God. Let us remember the truth of Psalm 46:10: "Be still, and know that I am God."

The Good News of Christ

By God's grace and mighty power, I have been given the
privilege of serving him by spreading this Good News.

~ Ephesians 3:7 NLT

Once you have been born again, you are changed from
the inside out. If a person has not been born again,
they will never accomplish what the Bible calls them to
do. We need the power of the Holy Spirit in our lives.

It's the love of Christ in us that prompts us to preach
the Good News to others. Jeremiah 20:9 says, "His word
was in my heart like a burning fire shut up in my bones;
I was weary of holding it back, and I could not."

Remember, the Gospel always leads to acts. Once you
have heard the Gospel of Jesus Christ and you have
received salvation, been forgiven for all your sins and
found freedom from your past, you cannot wait to tell
others that Jesus Christ saves.

Once you've heard the salvation message, you can't help
but share it with those around you – you would feel it
is your moral duty to tell them there is a better way that
brings joy and peace.

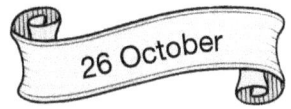

The Lord's Treasured Possession

If anyone speaks, let him speak as the oracles of God. If anyone ministers, let him do it as with the ability which God supplies, that in all things God may be glorified through Jesus Christ.

~ 1 Peter 4:11

It warms God's heart when we speak about the Bible, share the Good News of Christ and speak words that are good, kind and build others up. I have been preaching the Gospel for many years, and it is only when the Word of God is spoken in its entirety, with conviction, belief and faith, that hearts are changed.

People do not get saved or come to salvation in God when a church service is like a comedy show. It's the Word of God that sets the captives free. As believers we need to speak life, which is the complete and undiluted Word of God.

When we speak the Word of God, it is as if Jesus is speaking and with that goes great power and anointing. The Bible is more than sufficient and in God's economy, there is no plan B; there is only one plan.

Let us simplify our preaching and our lifestyles, extend love to all people and speak about things that pertain to eternal life.

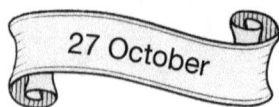

Appeasing the Crowd

Pilate said to them, "Why, what evil has He done?" But they cried out all the more, "Crucify Him!" So Pilate, wanting to gratify the crowd, released Barabbas to them; and he delivered Jesus, after he had scourged Him, to be crucified.

~ Mark 15:14-15

As Christians, we can no longer "appease the crowd". We have to come apart, and we must be different. We cannot say we love Jesus and continue to live as we did before we were saved.

Pontius Pilate saw that the carpenter from Nazareth had done nothing wrong. Yet because of his fear of the crowd, he simply washed his hands in a basin and told the soldiers to take Him away and crucify Him. Pontius compromised on doing the right thing.

There are too many Christians today who are wishy-washy, who would compromise on doing the right thing to make sure that the mob is happy. They are neither here nor there. When they speak, they speak like a politician. They don't stand up for anything and refuse to get involved or commit themselves to a cause.

When we start to speak the truth in love, however, then God will undertake for us; but as long as we keep compromising, I can tell you that we will find no favour with the Living God.

Give Thanks

Jesus answered and said, "Were there not ten cleansed? But where are the nine? Were there not any found who returned to give glory to God except this foreigner?" And He said to him, "Arise, go your way. Your faith has made you well."

~ Luke 17:17-19

Our country has suffered severe droughts. And yet many parts of our land have received some rain. We need to learn to say, "Thank You," to God for the rain in our lives. I'm not just talking about physical rain only but also about the spiritual blessings that come after extreme hardships. We need to be more grateful for God's blessings in our lives.

In Luke 17, we read that the Lord Jesus healed 10 lepers but only one, a Samaritan, came back to give thanks. How often do those whom we least expect to be grateful come and say thank you?

Something that has brought me much solace and peace is that whenever I am able to do something for someone, I choose to do it as unto the Lord. If there is no response, gratitude or thanks, I choose not to be offended. I am doing it for God, and not for the individual.

As Colossians 3:23 tells us, "Whatever you do, do it heartily, as to the Lord and not to men."

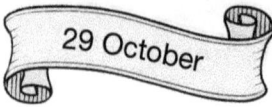

Who Is Jesus?

Christ also suffered for us, leaving us an example, that you should follow His steps: "Who committed no sin, nor was deceit found in His mouth."

~ 1 Peter 2:21-22

Jesus is God made flesh (see John 1:14). He is the Son of God, but Jesus is God also. Jesus said, "If you've seen Me, you've seen My Father" (John 14:9). The Bible confirms this many times (see John 12:45, Heb. 1:3, Col. 1:15, Phil. 2:6).

No one else has ever been raised from the dead like Jesus was. No human being has ever walked on water like Jesus did. He has no beginning, and no end.

Jesus asked Peter in Matthew 16:15-17, "But who do you say that I am?" Simon Peter replied, "You are the Christ, the Son of the living God." Jesus answered and said to him, "Blessed are you, Simon Bar-Jonah, for flesh and blood has not revealed this to you, but My Father who is in heaven."

Unless a person is born again, says John 3:3, they will never see the Kingdom of Heaven. We can see that Jesus is God when we see the change in the lives of people who have accepted Him as Lord and Saviour. The blind receive their sight, and the deaf hear in an instant when they meet Jesus, the Son of God.

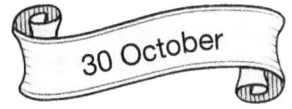

Receive the Mantle

Then he took the mantle of Elijah that had fallen from
him ...

~ 2 Kings 2:14

In 2 Kings 2, we read the story of Elijah's servant, Elisha,
wanting Elijah's mantle. In verse 14, because of his
continual persistence he eventually received the mantle.

God's calling on a person's life is much bigger than
anything that the person has ever done before. God
will give us something to do for Him that we cannot
handle in our own strength, because when we accomplish the mission, God can receive all the glory. The
average person can see that it was a move of God,
something that God Himself had orchestrated, which
we could never have done.

Many times in my life God has given me a directive
and I have said every time, "Lord, I cannot do it." Then
the Lord encouraged me and showed that He will do it
through me by His strength. And He has come through
for me every single time.

The prayer meetings that have taken place in South
Africa over the last few years are an example of this,
where multitudes of people have come together. These
meetings could never take place if it had not been a God-
directive. We need to do what He tells us and He will
surely make it possible.

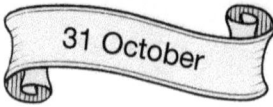

Draw Near to God

A man's heart plans his way, but the LORD directs his steps ... Honest weights and scales are the LORD's; all the weights in the bag are His work.

~ Proverbs 16:9, 11

In my mind's eye I can see an old-fashioned set of scales ... on the one side are trials and tribulations; on the other side, to balance the scale, are consolations.

Second Corinthians 1:5 tells us, "For as the sufferings of Christ abound in us, so our consolation also abounds through Christ." In other words, the Lord has promised you and me as Christians that the more tribulation or trials we go through, the more comfort He will give us.

Big hearts are made through big troubles. We know that character and compassion are developed when we go through trying times. Romans 5:3-4 says, "We also glory in tribulations, knowing that tribulation produces perseverance; and perseverance, character; and character, hope." It is through the hardships we endure that our personality and our character grow.

Keep trusting in God – He will help you rise above your circumstances: above your sadness, above your anxiety, above your loneliness, above your illness, above your difficulty. Remain close to the Lord and you will taste the victory.

November

In Him we have redemption through His blood,
the forgiveness of sins, according
to the riches of His grace.

~ Ephesians 1:7 ~

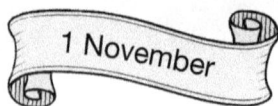

Are You with Him?

"I have said to you, 'You shall inherit their land, and I will give it to you to possess, a land flowing with milk and honey.' I am the Lord your God."

~ Leviticus 20:24

The Bible tells us very clearly in 2 Corinthians 5:17, "Therefore if anyone is in Christ, he is a new creation; old things have passed away; behold, all things have become new."

We need to leave the past and move on. Jesus states in Matthew 12:30, "He who is not with Me is against Me, and he who does not gather with Me scatters abroad."

There is no time to sit on the fence. It is time to let your "Yes" be "Yes", and your "No" be "No". Then we shall experience that blessed peace we are so desperately seeking after in this world. Of course, there will always be challenges to face, but God has given us people to help us and He is training us for future endeavours.

Jesus says, "These things I have spoken to you, that in Me you may have peace. In the world you will have tribulation; but be of good cheer, I have overcome the world" (John 16:33).

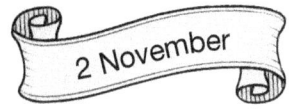

Our Father Always Hears

The LORD has heard my supplication; the LORD will receive my prayer.

~ Psalm 6:9

Referring to Psalm 6, Charles Spurgeon said, "The experience here recorded is mine." I agree with him wholeheartedly, for I too have had that same experience in my Christian journey. And the older I get, the sweeter my prayer life becomes. The evidence of answered prayer is just so real to me.

An important ingredient for prayer is desire. The great intercessor E. M. Bounds said, "Without desire, prayer is a meaningless mumble of words. Its exercise is a waste of precious time, and from it, no real blessing accrues." It's not how long or how often you pray, but faith and desire that make for effective prayer.

Keep a daily journal on what Jesus says to you through His Word. Then have your prayer time. You can use the ACTS formula – **A**doration, **C**onfession, **T**hanksgiving and **S**upplication. Speak to the Lord in the morning, as you wake up. Give Him the first fruits of the day. It will change your whole life.

You and I have to pray the prayer of faith and then have the patience to wait for the answer – because it will come!

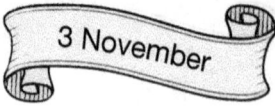

Arise, Shine!

Arise, shine; for your light has come! And the glory of the Lord is risen upon you. For behold, the darkness shall cover the earth, and deep darkness the people; but the Lord will arise over you, and His glory will be seen upon you.

~ Isaiah 60:1-2

It is time to wake up out of our sleep and to let our lights shine just as the Lord tells us to! Even as the darkness is covering the earth, we are to shine even brighter for Jesus and, of course, for the lost, the blind and those who have no hope.

We cannot afford to compromise our faith for the benefit of popularity in the eyes of the world. For it will only diminish our brightness. The fear of man causes the dullness. If we allow Jesus to shine through us, then unbelievers and even the leaders of this sad, lost world will be drawn to us like a moth to a flame in the midst of the darkness. Quite simply because they will want what we have: godly peace, hope, vision and godly love. How the world desperately seeks after these things!

Let us allow Jesus to so shine through us that the lost souls of this world will be led to the Prince of Peace.

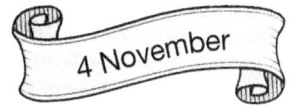

Rebuild the Ruins

They shall rebuild the old ruins, they shall raise up the former desolations, and they shall repair the ruined cities, the desolations of many generations.

~ Isaiah 61:4

It's time to bring into reality the principles of God that have been eroded over time and compromised. God Himself is doing this and He is using the ordinary people of this world to help Him!

God is using the farmer, the businessman, the artisan, the builder and the school teacher. When you give yourself to Jesus, say, "Lord, I can't do this alone. I can't go on alone." That's what Peter, Moses and David said. And the Lord will say, "Now I can use you." Our God is the God of the down-and-outs.

The desolations of many generations will be restored by God and the nations will see it. Worldly people will see the different lifestyle of children belonging to the Lord and they'll be drawn to it: God is calling forth a holy people who will stand for truth and righteousness and who will not be ashamed to call sin by its name. Thank God today for never giving up on His people.

By His grace He saved you and He will give you the strength you need to do Kingdom work for Him.

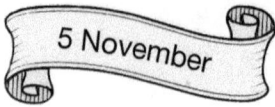

Not a Word

But He answered him not one word, so that the governor marveled greatly.

~ Matthew 27:14

Sometimes mouthing off is not such a good idea. It is often more effective to hold our tongues when, as Christians, we are criticised for our faith or our actions. It is not easy, but often more impactful than shouting for all to hear in an attempt to defend the name of our Lord Jesus. This will only put people off Jesus, instead of drawing them closer to Him.

Negative spoken words or curses can be broken by the Word of God, which speaks light and life. There is dynamic power in the spoken Word. I encourage you to use the gifts God has given you to use words so that you can have a fulfilled life in Christ.

Begin to speak life, not only over other people, but over yourself as well. David often did that: "Why are you cast down, O my soul?" (Ps. 43:5). Start speaking about the good attributes that God has given you. He's given you so many gifts. Acknowledge them and use them today.

Let your words be few and let your actions speak loudly of the Almighty God you follow.

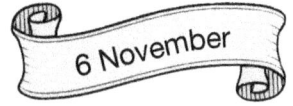

A Tribute to Mothers

Her children rise up and call her blessed; her husband also, and he praises her.

~ Proverbs 31:28

We thank God for our mothers. Where would we be without them? My late mother was probably my single biggest encouragement before I met my wife. When others didn't have a kind word to say about me, my mother always stood up for me.

John Wesley said that out of all the theologians he had studied under in Europe, men of high calibre like John Calvin and Count Zinzendorf who started the Moravian Church, his mother, Susanna, was the greatest influence in his life.

They say that the man is the head of the house, but the mother is definitely the heart of the home. Having travelled all across the globe, I can feel the presence of a godly mother when I walk through the front door of a house. It is not wealth that touches my heart, it is the love and the presence of God in the mother's heart that really makes me feel at home.

When Jesus was on the cross, He said to His mother and the disciple standing nearby: "'Woman, behold your son!' Then He said to the disciple, 'Behold your mother!'" (John 19:26-27) Jesus uttered those words while in excruciating pain, yet He still had time enough to acknowledge a godly mother.

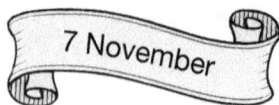

The Urgency of the Hour

"And this Gospel of the Kingdom shall be preached in all the world for a witness unto all nations; and then shall the end come."

~ Matthew 24:14

As I write today's devotion, I have a tremendous urgency in my spirit. People desperately need the Lord Jesus and His message of salvation.

The Lord did not say that He will come back when all of mankind is saved. He said that He will return when all of mankind has heard the Gospel message. God's Holy Word is to be completely trusted and followed. Jesus clearly states that Heaven and earth shall pass away, but His words shall by no means pass away (see Matt. 24:35).

This mandate from God is not only for evangelists and missionaries, but for every single believer – whether they are students, nursing mothers, sportsmen, teachers, farmers, politicians, children, or pensioners. We have all been called by Jesus to go out and spread the Gospel, to be His faithful witnesses (see Acts 1:8).

God bless you as you faithfully blow the trumpet and warn the people of His return. Meditate on the words of Hebrews 9:28 today: "To those who eagerly wait for Him He will appear a second time."

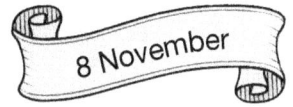

Freedom in Christ

Stand fast therefore in the liberty by which Christ has made us free, and do not be entangled again with a yoke of bondage.

~ Galatians 5:1

Jesus says that if He sets you free, you will be free indeed (see John 8:36).

Our worst enemy, preventing us from true freedom in Christ, is ourselves! That's right. We are all that stands in the way of us and the freedom Jesus offers. The apostle Paul recognised this and he was set free through Christ's power in him. In Galatians 2:20, he says, "I have been crucified with Christ; it is no longer I who live, but Christ lives in me; and the life which I now live in the flesh I live by faith in the Son of God, who loved me and gave Himself for me."

Freedom is not something we can achieve in our own strength. Only the sovereign work of God can set us free. With that freedom comes liberty and we find that reverence for God replaces the fear of man in our hearts.

We acknowledge Him as greater than ourselves. As we come to know God's love, we can reach beyond ourselves to love others.

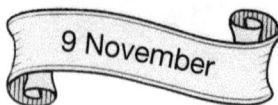

Shout it From the Rooftops

"Therefore whoever confesses Me before men, him I will also confess before My Father who is in heaven. But whoever denies Me before men, him I will also deny before My Father who is in heaven."

~ Matthew 10:32-33

People need the Lord Jesus like never before. For many, they will only ever hear the Gospel in the way we as Christians act and talk!

The Message puts it straight in Matthew 10:26-27, "Don't be intimidated. Eventually everything is going to be out in the open, and everyone will know how things really are. So don't hesitate to go public now."

Don't be bluffed into silence by the threats of bullies. There's nothing they can do to your soul. Save your fear for God, who holds your entire existence in His hands.

God baptizes us in His Holy Spirit so that we will be bold and so full of love, grace, mercy and compassion that we will tell the whole world what the Lord has done for us. I cannot wait to go to distant countries and tell people about Jesus, encouraging them and reminding them how much God loves them. Of course, I need power to do that and that power comes from the Holy Spirit.

Let us tell the whole world that Jesus is Lord!

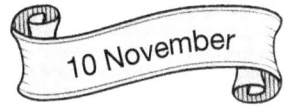

He Is Risen

He is risen! He is not here.

~ Mark 16:6

On a beautiful crisp autumn morning, I listened to the singing of the birds in the trees just outside my quiet time room. There was not a breath of wind blowing outside. It was as if the angels from Heaven reminded me that all is well, for Christ has risen. He has risen indeed.

He is not in the grave; He is very much alive and I can feel His presence with me as I write today.

Having had the great privilege of going to Israel many times and visiting the tomb, I can assure you that it's empty. There is nothing in it – no bones, no grave cloths, nothing! You can also visit King David's tomb, whose remains are still very much there.

Jesus is not a historical figure. It's not like reading about Alexander the Great or Napoleon Bonaparte, because Jesus Christ is not in the grave. He's alive and well and He's listening to your heart conversing with Him as you are reading this book right now.

Enjoy today, knowing that if Christ Jesus is for us then no one will stand against us (see Rom. 8:31).

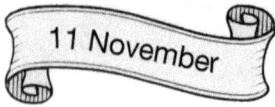

Settle Your Differences

"Moreover if your brother sins against you, go and tell him his fault between you and him alone. If he hears you, you have gained your brother."

~ Matthew 18:15

We really need to settle our differences. Then we will start to feel the reward that comes from obedience; the peace and joy that we receive from God when hearing and obeying His will for our lives. I can hear you saying, "But, it was not my fault! I didn't do anything wrong. She did it. He did it ... "

The Lord Jesus clearly says, "If your brother sins against you ... " Jesus knows what is good for you and me. He knows that unforgiveness can turn into hatred and bitterness.

Embrace the freedom of forgiveness. God has forgiven us so much and we are called to do the same for those who have hurt us. God sets the example in 1 John 1:9 where we're told very clearly that if we confess our sins, we'll be cleansed of all unrighteousness. God is more than happy to meet us where we are.

Let's go swiftly to that person who has trespassed against us (often very close to home) and tell them what it is that has offended you. Make up, so that Jesus can take the burden off of you.

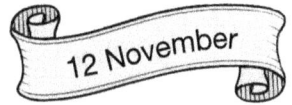

How Far?

"And whoever compels you to go one mile, go with him two."

~ Matthew 5:41

The question God is asking you today is how far are you prepared to go for His Son?

Or, put it this way, how far did the Son of God go for you? We know the answer all too well. He went all the way, even to the Cross of Calvary. Jesus says in John 15:13 (KJV), "Greater love hath no man than this, that a man lay down his life for his friends."

We have to go the whole way for our fellow man, especially the poor, the needy, the old and the infirm, the widow and the orphan, the gangster and the alcoholic, the prostitute and the drug addict.

The question today is not: What's in it for me when I follow Jesus? The question is rather: What can I do today to proclaim Jesus and win people for Him, even though it may cost me my life? Surrender your life to Christ. Then it is no longer you who lives, but Christ who lives in you (see Gal. 2:20).

God bless you as you allow the Holy Spirit to speak to your heart about going the extra mile for others.

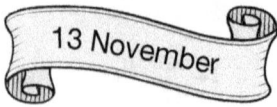

God Is in Control

In the multitude of my anxieties within me, Your comforts delight my soul.

~ Psalm 94:19

One of my spiritual sons sent me this quote: "Worry is like a rocking chair. It gives you something to do, but it doesn't get you anywhere." How true is that.

The Lord wants to remind us once again today that He is indeed in full control of everything happening in and around us. In Revelation 1:8, we read: "'I am the Alpha and the Omega, the Beginning and the End,' says the Lord, 'who is and who was and who is to come, the Almighty.'"

Jesus Christ is in full control of this world even though some of us might think everything is spinning out of control.

Be encouraged today and remember that the Lord is still in control. He's in control not only of every aspect of our lives, but of everything that happens on this earth. At the end of the day, we're waiting for that final spring day, the day when the Lord will come to take us home to be with Him in glory. But until that day, enjoy smelling the roses, enjoy God's creation and thank Him, not only for the big things, but also for the little things in life.

Our Hope of Glory

I have fought the good fight, I have finished the race, I have kept the faith.

~ 2 Timothy 4:7

I recently read something very interesting that was written by one of South Africa's top sports scientists. He wrote that for the 35 years he had been studying human anatomy, he had come to realise that one has to be physically strong and in shape to take part in a race. Yet, at the end of the day, it is believing in oneself and one's ability to get it done that will carry one across the finish line. I want to add something here – it is only Christ in us that is our hope of glory (see Col. 1:27).

Paul talks about physical exercise being of some benefit, but ultimately it is spiritual fitness – spending time in the presence of God – that will help us to finish the race and win the victor's crown. May God bless you as you continue to work hard by keeping yourself in shape physically and, more importantly, spiritually.

Let us finish the race in the Spirit, as we started it the day we met God. How do we do that? By spending time reading the Word of God, praying and having fellowship with other Christians.

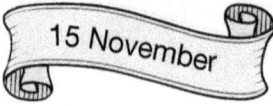

In an Instant

To this you were called, because Christ also suffered for us, leaving us an example, that you should follow His steps.

~ 1 Peter 2:21

When Jesus called His disciples to follow after Him, they left their fishing nets and followed Him *immediately* (see Matt. 4:18-22). As a direct result of their instant obedience, those Galilean fishermen witnessed the greatest move of God in the history of the world!

We need to be sensitive to the call of God. We cannot be found to be procrastinating.

On one trip to Israel I went to Capernaum. I was on the shores of Lake Galilee. I could visualize those fishermen fishing there – a settled lifestyle. Even the future of their children was planned out.

Then, all of a sudden, Jesus is standing next to them. He shakes every single thing they've ever done. He says, "Leave those fishing nets. You will no longer catch fish. From now on you will be fishers of men."

There is no time to waste as the coming of the Lord Jesus draws ever nearer. Proverbs 6:10-11 says, "A little sleep, a little slumber, a little folding of the hands to sleep – so shall your poverty come on you like a prowler, and your need like an armed man."

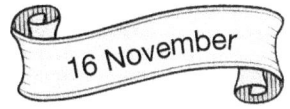

Count to Ten

Whoever guards his mouth and tongue keeps his soul from troubles.

~ Proverbs 21:23

As we fast approach the end of the year, it is very evident that people are tired, quite impatient and rather bothered. This is a time when we as followers of Jesus need to be extremely patient and gentle, extending a lot of grace to others.

It is a wonderful time of year to show our true colours in the busy shopping malls, on the roads where the traffic is hectic and while waiting in long queues. Godliness with contentment is great gain (see 1 Tim. 6:6).

I believe that the Lord wants us to refrain from speaking too much. It is stated clearly in Proverbs that the more we speak, the more likely we are to get ourselves into trouble. We are to let our lives speak for us.

We need to count to ten before we say something that might be hurtful or counterproductive. Because you'll have a better chance of not saying that nasty thing and by so doing prevent an ugly or hurtful situation.

A kind and thoughtful word can literally change someone's life. Jesus said that we are to love one another as He has loved us (see John 15:12).

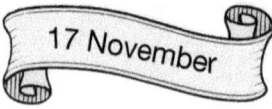

A Rogue Wave

He calmed the storm to a whisper and stilled the waves.

~ Psalm 107:29 NLT

I read a book by Bob Buford recently titled *Halftime*. In it he discusses the different challenges in life and speaks about the rogue wave that hits your sail boat when you least expect it. Can you imagine going out to sea on your boat … it's a sunny day and everything is peaceful … then out of nowhere comes a huge wave that shatters the peace.

Maybe your rogue wave is called drought or a death in the family. Bob talks about his own rogue wave, the death of his only son. His son was 24 years old and very successful in all areas of his life. He was a God-fearing man with lots of friends and he lived life to the full. He went down to the Rio Grande River with two friends and they tried to swim across. Unfortunately, he drowned. Bob writes that he was absolutely devastated when this rogue wave hit him.

I have had a number of rogue waves in my life. It's painful when it is so very close to home and we don't seem to have the answer. If you're facing a rogue wave at this time, hand it over to Jesus. He will take care of it.

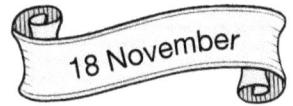

Strength for the Strain

The LORD will give strength to His people; the LORD will bless His people with peace.

~ Psalm 29:11

Years ago we travelled in our yellow truck, called the Seed Sower, to spread the Gospel from Cape Town to Cairo. I was sitting on the banks of the mighty Zambezi River one day. We couldn't use the bridge, so we had to cross the mighty river on a pontoon. There was a backlog of massive trucks and ours was stuck right in the middle of the queue. I felt very homesick. Once we'd crossed the Zambezi, it was six weeks until we headed home. But the Lord, through the power of His Holy Spirit, gave me His peace.

Charles Spurgeon said, "That same God who rides upon the storm in days of tempest will also rule the hurricane of our tribulation and send us, before long, days of peace. We shall have strength for storms and songs for fair weather. Away, dark thoughts! Up faith and hope!"

As I started praying and waiting on the Lord, my strength was indeed renewed.

No matter what you are going through right now, remember the Lord is with you and He will deliver you. You will have ample opportunity to praise Him for His goodness.

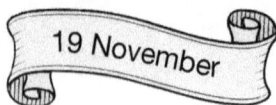

A Purpose for Life

I cry out to God Most High, to God who will fulfill His purpose for me.

~ Psalm 57:2 NLT

John Newton could not find peace or purpose in life. His job was hell. He was the captain of a slave ship. But then he met Jesus Christ in an incredible and personal way and his life was transformed in a moment. He wrote the beloved hymn: "Amazing Grace! How sweet the sound that saved a wretch like me! I once was lost, but now am found; was blind, but now I see."

When you meet Jesus Christ, you don't have to work to gain inner peace; you don't have to study; you don't have to pass an exam. You just have to have faith and believe in Him and then that peace which I'm talking about will come upon you in a most dramatic way.

The peace comes about when you acknowledge that the Man from Nazareth, Jesus Christ, died for all of your sins and you now have freedom and eternal life. John 14:27 says, "Peace I leave with you, My peace I give to you; not as the world gives do I give to you. Let not your heart be troubled, neither let it be afraid."

Who Are You in Christ?

But as many as received Him, to them He gave the right to become children of God, to those who believe in His name.

~ John 1:12

One of the most important requirements for a successful Christian life is to know who you are in Christ. A while ago, while reading the Word of God, He impressed upon me Judges 8:21, which says, "For as a man is, so is his strength."

That statement was not made by a child of God. In fact, it was made by the enemy. Two Midianite kings were captured by Gideon, who said to his son Jether, "Kill them." But Jether was afraid and did not take his sword out of its sheath. It was then that the two kings said to Gideon, "For as a man is, so is his strength."

When you know who you are in Christ, you will attempt great and mighty things for the Lord. However, when you don't spend time with God and you forget the authority and the power that He has given you, you become weak. If you keep bringing yourself down, you will become a failure.

But if you start to speak the Word of God over yourself and believe what He says about you, nothing will hold you back.

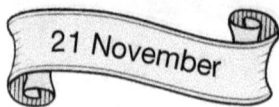

Take Time Out

Then Jesus said, "Let's go off by ourselves to a quiet place and rest awhile."

~ Mark 6:31 NLT

When we get too busy we lose compassion for our fellow men. In fact, our heart starts to become hard and that is just what the devil wants. He wants us to be distracted and so worn out with our own concerns that we don't care about others.

If we are so busy that we lose our heart for others, we are on a downward spiral. I believe that this was what was happening to the disciples when Jesus said to them: "'Come aside by yourselves to a deserted place and rest a while' For there were many coming and going, and they did not even have time to eat. So they departed to a deserted place in the boat by themselves" (Mark 6:31-32).

Sit under a nice shady tree and watch the sun set with your loved ones. Take time to greet the car guard; stop and help the elderly lady carry her groceries. It is easy to forget what it really is that God has called us for in this world: to be His ambassadors. Jesus was never too busy for people. Make time for others today.

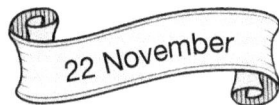

Comfort in His Companionship

"Forty years You sustained them in the wilderness; they lacked nothing; their clothes did not wear out and their feet did not swell."

~ Nehemiah 9:21

We need to spend more time with Jesus and get direction from Him. We need to stop resisting the Lord and hardening our hearts like the Israelites did in the desert.

Every time the going got tough, they complained. They even tried to stone Moses because things were not going well. As a result, it took them forty years to reach the Promised Land. The Lord had to take them around the mountain in order to chasten them, because He loved them.

If we allow the Lord to lead us as He led the Israelites, we will lack nothing. In this day and age where all things are questionable, we need the comfort and compassion of Jesus Christ.

If we walk in companionship with Him, He will direct every step of the way and we will have nothing to fear. He has promised that He will never leave nor forsake us! (see Heb. 13:5). We just need to be sure that we do not leave Him.

By getting up early every morning and having your quiet time with God, you will ensure that your day goes well.

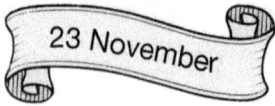

Speak Up!

"If I perish, I perish!"

~ Esther 4:16

Queen Esther was committed to speaking the truth in love and we know how her story ended. She stood in the gap for the Jewish nation and prevented a possible genocide from taking place.

We need to speak up. We cannot afford to keep quiet. This country of ours is hanging in the balance and the Word of God has the answer: "Sanctify [set them apart] them by Your truth. Your word is truth" (John 17:17). The truth. We have to be different from the world. If we are going to be outspoken, it needs to be in word and deed. Queen Esther was prepared to be different. She came apart and she spoke the truth to the king and that changed his mind.

We have all been called by God and we need to do our part so that God can do His part. When believers stand up and speak the truth in love, we will see a complete turnaround in this nation.

May God bless you as you start to shine as a light, first in your own home, then in your town, then in your province and then in the nation.

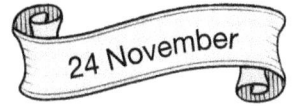

Turn Back to God

Husbands, love your wives, just as Christ also loved the church and gave Himself for her.

~ Ephesians 5:25

A while ago, I had the privilege of revisiting the different Mighty Men gatherings in South Africa. My heart is excited about what God is doing.

Men are seeking after God like never before. I really believe that a worldwide revival is possible if men are willing to step up to their responsibilities in the home, in the workplace, on the sports field and in the learning centres of the world.

I am seeing men's hearts of stone softened. That is a sign that God is working in and through their lives. Even as we see situations deteriorating throughout the world, especially in the area of immorality in the home, lack of respect and submission, we are also seeing God calling His soldiers to report for duty. Like never before we are going to have to stand up for what the Word of God says without compromise.

In South Africa, I see a healthy future as men of all races and cultures come together, unite and stand on God's Holy Word. Keep it simple and do not compromise your faith for anyone. May God bless you as you continue to make a stand for Him.

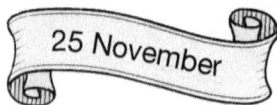

Be Reconciled

If we confess our sins, He is faithful and just to forgive us our sins and to cleanse us from all unrighteousness.

~ 1 John 1:9

On occasion I have been asked about how we can encourage reconciliation. It is very simple: We need to talk to each other and be kind. That will ignite reconciliation. It does not happen in Parliament, or by signing a paper that declares that we shall be reconciled. It starts in the home between husband and wife, father and son, mother and daughter, and then spreads out to the neighbourhood, the district and then eventually into the whole nation.

Reconciliation starts at ground level. We need to talk to God. He reconciled us to Himself by sending us His only begotten Son who became the Reconciler between man and God.

Reconciliation begins when people talk to each other. You say that people won't listen. Keep talking, eventually they will hear. You say I can't forgive. Well, you have to because God forgave you. The Lord says that if you can't love your brother whom you can see, how can you love God whom you cannot see (see 1 John 4:20)?

Start now and take the first step towards reconciliatation.

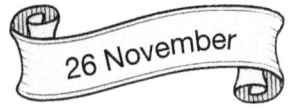

Times Are Changing

"Now learn a lesson from the fig tree. When its branches bud and its leaves begin to sprout, you know that summer is near. In the same way, when you see all these things, you can know His return is very near, right at the door."

~ Matthew 24:32-33 NLT

The signs of the times are all around us. Things are constantly changing and we need to adapt. Never compromise God's Word. Remain strong by spending time in prayer, reading your Bible and having fellowship with other believers.

We need to choose which way we want to go, because change always requires a decision. Joshua 24:15 says, "Choose for yourselves this day whom you will serve … But as for me and my house, we will serve the LORD." Joshua was such a great leader, because he was not indecisive. As things changed, he adapted.

The way we adapt is by walking closely with the Master. He has promised not to leave us as orphans (see John 14:18). He will direct us and, if we fall behind, we will not lose our way. He will come to us and help us (see Isa. 41:10).

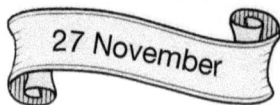

Do Your Part

All the people went their way to eat and drink, to send portions and rejoice greatly, because they understood the words that were declared to them.

~ Nehemiah 8:12

It is very important for God's people to come together in one place (see Neh. 8:1) to hear and understand the Word of God. It must be conveyed simply, yet powerfully.

Nehemiah 8:4 says that Ezra the scribe stood on a platform, opened the Book of the Law and read from it. The people said, "Amen, Amen," and worshipped the Lord (see Neh. 8:6). When Ezra read God's Word, it made sense and it helped the people to understand His purpose. They went away with joy and strength, because they had heard from the Lord.

God has given me clear instructions over the years on what I need to do. He wants to see different racial groups and age groups coming together in one place to hear the undiluted Word of God spoken simply and clearly. Once having received the mandate, it's important to respond to it and then to leave the rest in His hands.

That is why the Israelites left the meeting worshipping the Lord, because they had done what God had told them to do. Let us be obedient to Him, allowing God do His part as we do our part.

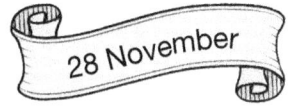

Our Compass

In the beginning was the Word, and the Word was with God, and the Word was God.

~ John 1:1

My greatest concern amongst God's people at this moment is compromise and heresy within the fold.

Jesus warns us to be careful of wolves who parade around in sheep's clothing. I've heard international Christian leaders saying that the Bible is of no relevance or influence anymore in society. Hearing such things concerns me deeply. Especially when it comes to young people who are seeking godly direction.

The truth is, if you take the Bible out of the equation, you have nothing left. Everything we believe and everything we stand for comes from God's Word.

First John 5:7 says, "For there are three that bear witness in heaven: the Father, the Word, and the Holy Spirit; and these three are one." Jesus Christ is, in fact, the Word and the Word is Christ.

The legacy which I am determined to leave is the importance and relevance of God's Word, because when everything else falls away, God's Word will stand (see Isa. 40:8).

In the Word of God, we have everything we need. The Word of God is our compass, our GPS for life.

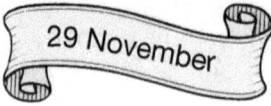

Train Your Children

Train up a child in the way he should go, and when he is old he will not depart from it.

~ Proverbs 22:6

A father wears many hats. He is the vet, the electrician, the builder, the plumber, the mechanic, the accountant, but he is also the head of the home. He must make sure that his children grow up to fear God.

How do we protect our children against the onslaught of the devil? When considering social media and everything our children are exposed to, it is almost as if evil is seeking out our children more and more.

There is only one way to raise godly children and that is through the Word of God. It is our responsibility to bring up God-fearing children. It is not for the school teacher, the sports master, or even a counsellor to bring them up. Your children will not do what you tell them, they will do exactly what you do.

At the end of the day, we just need to ask ourselves one question: What would Jesus do? We have to major in God's Word, His love, His power, His strength and His promise of eternal life. Then we will start to think more clearly, operate more rationally and taste godly success as parents.

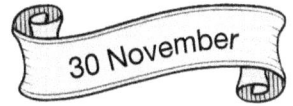

Bring the Good News

Deliver my soul, O Lord, from lying lips and from a deceitful tongue.

~ Psalm 120:2

To exaggerate is a way of getting attention and dramatizing events to evoke a response. Yet the truth always comes out and the storyteller is exposed as a liar.

As Christians, I believe we have a responsibility to walk in the Spirit of Truth and to make sure that the facts we convey to others are correct. We are not here to fan the flames of chaos and turmoil. We are here to pray for and to intercede on behalf of those who don't know Jesus, yet desperately need His saving grace.

Our country is filled with wonderful opportunities. Of course we have challenges, what country doesn't? The world over, countries are facing challenges of increasing magnitude. People are suffering the effect of wars, famine and earthquakes, multiplied by lawlessness and iniquity.

There is hatred, fear, confusion and turmoil in the hearts of many people. That is why God has told us to love and to bring the Gospel of salvation and peace to the lost. Let's be bearers of good news.

December

The Lord is compassionate and merciful,
slow to get angry and filled with unfailing love.

~ *Psalm 103:8* NLT ~

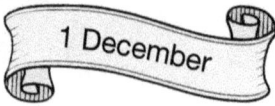

A Gentle Answer

A soft answer turns away wrath, but a harsh word stirs up anger.

~ Proverbs 15:1

Early one morning while praying, I felt the Holy Spirit direct me to read John 8. It's the story of the adulterous woman and the Pharisees. They brought a woman caught in adultery to Jesus, not primarily for justice, but to try and catch out the Lord so that they could eventually accuse Him and kill Him.

Often harsh words are a cover up for other underlying issues. The Pharisees came to Jesus and said, "According to the Law of Moses this woman should be stoned, because she was caught in adultery, but what do You say?" Jesus stooped down and wrote on the ground with His finger (we don't know what exactly He wrote, but He was very calm). They continued to provoke and question Him. Eventually He said, "He who is without sin among you, let him throw a stone at her first" (John 8:7). Then He bent down again to write on the ground.

Jesus asked the woman, "Where are your accusers?" She said, "There are none!" He replied, "I don't accuse you either, go and sin no more! Your sins are forgiven." We need to watch what we say. A harsh word hurts. A wise word will promote calm interactions. May the Lord bless you as you follow in His footsteps.

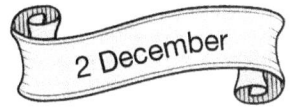

Act Promptly

And it shall be, when you hear the sound of marching in the tops of the mulberry trees, then you shall advance quickly. For then the Lord will go out before you to strike the camp of the Philistines.

~ 2 Samuel 5:24

I read in my quiet time just the other day about the importance of being ready for the move of the Holy Spirit. Jesus is the Master of the wind and the Maker of the rain. I experienced it personally once with 5,000 delegates from all over the world at Ein Gedi, at the Dead Sea. The place where David was hiding from King Saul. It was an evening meeting and we called upon the Lord to bring about revival. Suddenly a mighty rushing wind blew through the meeting. It started to rain on one of the lowest points on earth. It was an absolute miracle.

Our actions must be prompt and vigorous. We cannot determine the wind and we cannot make the rain, but what we can do is put the sail up on our boats so that when the wind comes, it will fill the sails to take us to our destination.

We need to be ready and wait on God in faith. Jesus says, "These things I have spoken to you, that in Me you may have peace. In the world you will have tribulation; but be of good cheer, I have overcome the world" (John 16:33).

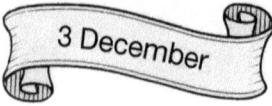

All Things for His Glory …

All things work together for the good of those who love the Lord and are called according to His purpose.

~ Romans 8:28

I have been severely tested in my walk with God. I even reached a point where I asked, "Lord, where are You?" But straight after that I have repented, because if you count your blessings and you see how far you've come, you will understand that none of us have any grounds to ask a question like that. God has never let me down. He has never forsaken you or me, no matter how you are feeling.

The Lord never promised us moonshine and roses when we committed our lives to Him. Psalm 34:19 says, "Many are the afflictions of the righteous, but the Lord delivers him out of them all."

If we look at the life of our beloved Saviour, He was not spared any affliction. Neither were His disciples. In fact, not one of them died of old age. They were martyred or died prematurely, but the good news is that the Lord will not leave us alone in our time of testing.

In the times of my greatest turmoil and onslaught from the evil one, the Master has been closest to me. May God bless you as you continue to run the race for Jesus.

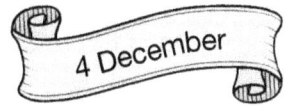

When Things Are Too Easy

Now in my prosperity I said, "I shall never be moved."
~ Psalm 30:6

When all is well, health, finance, business and family, it is very easy to forget our dependence on the Lord. A full barn makes one reluctant to get on one's knees and pray for help. But when the barn is empty, we quickly seek the face of God.

The world-famous heavyweight boxing champion Jack Dempsey became the champion of the world in the 1930s, the days of the great depression in America. He said that it was very easy for him to get up in the morning and do his training, jogging, and weightlifting when he was sleeping on a concrete floor. But when he became a world champion and dressed in a silk gown, it was much harder to be disciplined.

Continued worldly prosperity can be a fiery trial for the believer, because, "afflictions, though they seem severe, in mercy, are often sent." Adversity develops character. Therefore, we need to thank God for good times and for wonderful opportunities and holidays, but at the same time we need to be vigilant, for that is probably when God's children are the most vulnerable.

Stand strong and call out to God, especially during the good times.

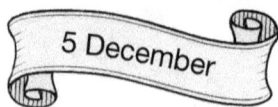

God Restores

Restore me, and I will return, for You are the LORD my God.
~ Jeremiah 31:18

Our God is in the restoration business. To restore simply means to give something that was stolen or removed back to the original owner.

That's exactly what God does for us. He restores that which moth and rust destroyed. Restoration is the nature of God. C. S. Lewis said, "If I find in myself a desire which no experience in this world can satisfy … I was made for another world." We are not of this world. There is an insatiable emptiness and hunger in our souls that only the love of God can fill. It is only hope in Jesus Christ that can restore that emptiness.

I remember as a brand-new Christian, over 40 years ago, listening to an American speaker saying, "You will never make a racehorse out of a donkey." Even as a new believer that did not sit well with me as I see myself very much as a donkey. In fact, as an early preacher they used to call me *Bongolo*. The word *imbongolo* is the Zulu for donkey. I'm actually honoured by this title as it was a donkey that carried the Master into Jerusalem and carried Mary to Bethlehem.

Turn back to the Restorer and let Him renew your life. Let God make a champion racehorse out of you, for His glory.

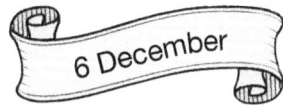

Always Be Grateful

Let the peace of God rule in your hearts, to which also you were called in one body; and be thankful.

~ Colossians 3:15

William Tiptaft once said, "God is pleased with gratitude because He gets so little of it."

Let's not take God's blessings for granted, because not one of us deserves anything from God. Instead of saying, "It's not enough", let us rather say, "God, thank You for giving us the life support we need by sending us what we need."

By telling others that Jesus Christ is Lord and that nothing can happen to us without His permission, is modelling Him to the world.

Job is a good example of a grateful person. He was not a fair-weather Christian. He refused to speak badly about God even when his wife asked him, "Why don't you curse God and die?" Job lost everything, but still he said, "Though He slay me, yet will I trust Him" (13:15).

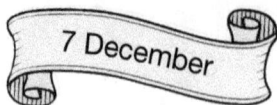

Obedience Leads to Holiness

Behold, the fear of the Lord, that is wisdom, and to depart
from evil is understanding.

~ Job 28:28

Holiness is the end product of obedience. When we are
holy people we are obedient people. The one doesn't
work without the other.

C. S. Lewis, in his book *The Lion* (representing Jesus),
the Witch (representing the devil) *and the Wardrobe,*
said of the lion, "He is not a tame lion … but a good
one."

The Bible tells us that God is a consuming fire (see Heb.
12:29) and Hebrews 12:14 says, "Pursue peace with all
people, and holiness, without which no one will see
the Lord." It concerns me deeply when I see the lack of
reverence for our Almighty God. He is a good God, but
He must be feared. The way you and I can prove to Him
that we respect Him is by obeying His commandments.

Hebrews 4:14-16 tells us that He is familiar with
our hardships, temptations and the challenges we
face on earth, because when He walked on this earth
Jesus Himself was subjected to every one of them. He
understands our situation and is very compassionate
towards His children. However, we must seek to do His
will above all else, and not follow our own way.

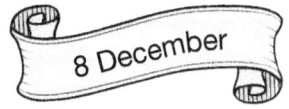

Honesty Goes a Long Way

We have renounced the hidden things of shame, not walking in craftiness nor handling the word of God deceitfully, but by manifestation of the truth commending ourselves to every man's conscience in the sight of God.

~ 2 Corinthians 4:2

Charles Swindoll said that honesty has a beautiful and refreshing simplicity about it. It is so uplifting to hear honest speech, see a clean lifestyle and to witness self-sacrifice without any ambitious undertones.

Like never before people want the truth plain and simple. The Lord will persevere with us as long as we are honest with Him. He longs to forgive us all our trespasses, shortfalls and mistakes if we come clean with Him and are honest about it.

I don't know how many times I have said to my children, "Just tell the truth." Honesty has such a clean way about it. In a world that is so corrupt, dishonest, and filled with personal gain, how delightfully refreshing to hear someone speak the truth honestly and plainly. That is what the church and the whole world seek after.

A. W. Tozer said, "Honesty that can be trusted and respected is a very fragrant flower in the life of the Christian." Let us keep our word.

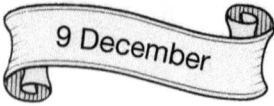

Meditate on It!

Meditate on these things; give yourself entirely to them, that your progress may be evident to all.

~ 1 Timothy 4:15

When we meditate we have an opportunity to digest what God is trying to say to us. When we think on the words in the Bible it becomes clear how He wants us to live.

If we say that we don't have time to sit and meditate, then we are in deep trouble. Vance Harner said, "When we are too busy to sharpen the axe, then we are too busy." People once asked Abraham Lincoln, "If you had six hours to cut down a tree, how would you go about it?" He replied, "I would spend the first four hours sharpening the axe."

I often have people write to me about temptations in their lives. Some tell me that they have a problem with lust and yet they continue to engage in pornographic material. Josiah Holland said, "The mind grows on what it feeds on." If we don't meditate on God's Word, we leave the door wide open for all kinds of temptations from the world to enter in.

If we don't make time for reflection and thinking deeply on God's Word, we will never grow in our faith. May God bless you as you start to discipline yourself and meditate regularly on the precious promises and blessings in the Bible.

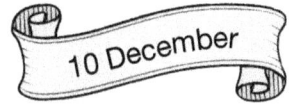

The Dark and Lonely Garden

"Stay here and watch with Me."

~ Matthew 26:38

We have been called on a mission that will take us to some dark places. Jesus promised that He would walk with us through the fire. He didn't say that He would remove the fire from the path. In fact, it's often through the fires of life that we learn many valuable lessons about being true followers of Christ.

Andrew Murray said, "By suffering the Father would lead us to enter more deeply into the love of Christ." Jesus literally sweat drops of blood in the Garden of Gethsemane, because He understood what was awaiting Him.

The cup of suffering is necessary if you and I are going to fulfil the call of God on our lives. Truth be told, we like to hear messages of prosperity, health, joy, success and victory. Yet as the saying goes, "No pain, no gain." The bigger the battle the greater the victory. We need to understand that we are in a battle on earth.

It is only in times of suffering that our faith is truly put to the test. I have said it before and I will say it again: I've never met a man or woman worth their salt who has not been through fiery trials. Trust God to see you through the difficult times.

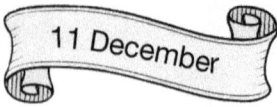

Pray Together

Praying always with all prayer and supplication in the Spirit, being watchful to this end with all perseverance and supplication for all the saints.

~ Ephesians 6:18

People often ask me what they can do for me before a big prayer meeting. My first and most urgent request to them is to please pray. Without prayer, I am wasting my time. When people pray God commands a great blessing (see Ps. 133).

I remember when, as a young farmer and believer, we suffered through a horrific drought season. I drove around my maize crop every day, watching it shrivel up. I cried out to the Lord, and I felt Him impressing upon me to host a prayer meeting in my hometown. I went to the mayor and asked him if I could use the town hall one Friday during lunchtime, and he agreed.

We came before the Lord that day from different denominations, areas and groups, and we prayed. When we left, the rain came pouring down. What an awesome God we serve. He is faithful. The answers will come, just persevere in prayer together.

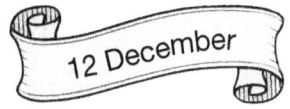

Trust in the Lord at All Costs

Some trust in chariots, and some in horses; but we will remember the name of the LORD our God.

~ Psalm 20:7

Today's Scripture verse is very clear about how we are supposed to live our lives. David slayed the giant Goliath because he trusted in the Lord. How ridiculous that a young shepherd boy could take on a skilled warrior. Goliath was notorious throughout the whole country. He was undefeated.

Yet sadly towards the end of David's life, he was the most powerful king with the greatest army in the Middle East, but decided to put his trust in man and not in God (see 1 Chronicles 21). David started off as a shepherd boy trusting God for everything, but when he grew older he put his trust in earthly things.

We need to finish the way we started. We need to trust God like never before. Then we will finish strong. Depend on the Holy Spirit to guide you, protect you and to be a friend who sticks closer than a brother.

May God bless you as you wait for His return. The Bible is so clear in Hebrews 11:6, "But without faith it is impossible to please Him, for he who comes to God must believe that He is, and that He is a rewarder of those who diligently seek Him."

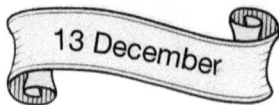

Finish the Job

Being confident of this very thing, that He who has begun a good work in you will complete it until the day of Jesus Christ.

~ Philippians 1:6

Times of hardship and testing will come. I am talking about drought, disease and political unrest. But we must be resolute and keep our eyes focused on our Lord. Luke 9:62 says, "No one, having put his hand to the plough, and looking back, is fit for the kingdom of God." Farmers know very well why! If you keep looking back you will never plough a straight line.

If God is on your side and you are serving Him with all your heart, He will ensure that you complete the job. You might be staring drought of some kind in the face as you read this, but God has a habit of taking a failure and turning it into a success.

In farming I have found many times that I have made more money through a dry year than through a year of abundance. Why? Because in the year of abundance everybody has a good crop and the price tends to plummet. But during a dry year when a lot of farmers have maybe not even planted, the price of the commodity soars. Even if you have an average crop, it can yield a great return. Continue in faith, and finish strong. God will finish in you what He has started. In His presence, even a negative situation will work out for the good of those who trust in Him.

A Solid Foundation

"Therefore whoever hears these sayings of Mine, and does them, I will liken him to a wise man who built his house on the rock."

~ Matthew 7:24

If there is one thing that agriculture has taught me from the start, it's that we can do our best, but unless God intervenes we have no future. Like the parable of the farmer who boasted of having a very large crop, so large that he could not store it in his barns and had to build bigger ones. He thought that everything else would also turn out well, until God said, "Tonight your soul will be required of you!"

God has no problem with success. In fact, a successful person who acknowledges God in his success brings a lot of joy to His heart.

Years ago a man built a beautiful house. He worked his whole life to build the house. He saved up his money and when the time came for him to retire, he got cancer and only lived there for three months before he died.

Make sure that you are not storing your treasures on earth. Focus on Jesus as your true foundation and build your life on Him. Then you will not be shaken.

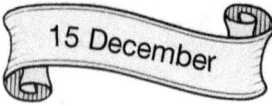

No Turning Back

Because you have kept My command to persevere, I also will keep you from the hour of trial which shall come upon the whole world, to test those who dwell on the earth.

~ Revelation 3:10

After the events of the Cross, the disciples were rather despondent. Peter said in John 21:3, "I am going fishing." And the rest of the disciples also went back to doing what they knew well.

Peter and the disciples went back to fishing on the Lake of Galilee. It's interesting that they fished all night but didn't catch anything.

Early the next morning Jesus stood on the shore and asked them this question, "Children, have you any food?" They answered Him, "No" (John 21:5). And He said to them, "Cast the net on the right side of the boat, and you will find some" (John 21:6). They did it and caught a multitude of fish. Then John realised that it was the Lord speaking to them, and Peter put on his outer garment and bailed over the side of the boat trying to get to Jesus.

When they all arrived at the shore, Jesus had already prepared breakfast for them. When we start to panic, we make foolish choices, which some of us will regret for the rest of our lives. Yet there is no going back for us. We are going on with the Lord and He will undertake for us in every circumstance.

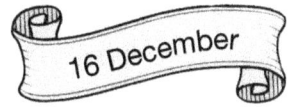

Life Is Short

All flesh is as grass, and all the glory of man as the flower of the grass. The grass withers, and its flower falls away, but the word of the LORD endures forever.

~ 1 Peter 1:24-25

Life on earth is short, and we must not take ourselves too seriously. The world will not stop turning when we're no longer around. I often smile when I see young people leaving school or university, and expecting the whole world to embrace them. Unfortunately, a rude awakening usually awaits them. You realise that people couldn't actually care less. So why are we here? It is to glorify God and enjoy Him forever (Westminster confession).

The Bible says, "Do not let the sun go down on your wrath" (Eph. 4:26). There should be no long faces before a family goes to bed at night. Life is short, and you don't know if you are to have another day on this earth, so don't waste time!

Conflict is always resolved by confrontation, unpleasant as it might be. So address problems and talk about them. Communicate – speak to your spouse, child, or colleague, and get to the bottom of the problem. Don't let things simmer and boil over. Once you've talked it through, you'll see there's no problem too big for God.

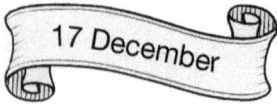

Walk Unashamed

But those who wait on the Lord shall renew their strength; they shall mount up with wings like eagles, they shall run and not be weary, they shall walk and not faint.

~ Isaiah 40:31

George Matheson once said, "Can you walk in white through the stained road ways of men? Can you touch the vile and polluted ones of earth, and retain your garments pure? Can you be in contact with the sinful and be yourself undefiled? If you can then you have surpassed the flight of the eagle."

If you can hold your head high when false accusations come against you, or if lies are spread about you, if people slander you and disrespect you for who you are, and you can still smile and forgive, then people will notice and will want what you have.

Like Matheson said, then you have surpassed the flight of the eagle. Our dependence should not be on the weather, or on what people dictate, or on the current political party. It should not be on any specific group of people, but our dependence should purely be on God and on Him alone.

Some of the most distinct memories I have of the past has not been so much about the successes during my time as a farmer, but actually during the toughest times. God always brings us through the storm, and the drought, if we just put our total trust and dependence in Him.

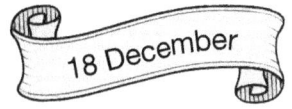

Watch Your Company

Evil company corrupts good habits.

~ 1 Corinthians 15:33

Your mind is a powerful thing. When you fill it with positive thoughts, your life will start to change for the better. We need to get alongside men and women who truly believe that there is a future for this country, and for all people.

If you look at Jesus' life, you will see that He spent a lot of time with the poor and the rich. In fact, Zacchaeus was convicted of his sin when Jesus visited his house, and he said that he would pay back four times the amount of money that he had stolen from the people. Then the Lord said, "Today salvation has come to this house" (Luke 19:9). There is no law in the Bible that convicts a man for being successful or for being wealthy.

There is a man I love to spend time with. He is over 80 and I have never heard a negative word come out of his mouth. When I once asked him, "What does the future hold for you?" He replied, "I have just completed building a high school and next year I want to start a first-year university." He is ploughing back and investing into the future of this nation. He is good company.

May God bless you as you spend time with men and women with godly habits and solid faith.

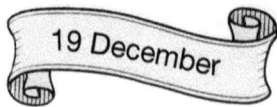

The Spider's Web

"He has always hated the truth, because there is no truth in him. When he lies, it is consistent with his character; for he is a liar and the father of lies."

~ John 8:44 NLT

The devil is the father of lies. He tries to catch us in a web of deceit and sin. A web is weaved by the spider to catch his prey, therefore we must stay well clear of any web that is weaved by the powers of darkness.

Remember, "There is therefore now no condemnation for those who are in Christ Jesus" (Rom. 8:1). The only thing the devil is capable of doing is accusing the brethren because he is the father of lies.

We need to remind ourselves what the Bible says – that if Christ is for us then there is no one that will stand against us (see Rom. 8:31).

Let us push the web aside and treat it with the contempt it deserves. Let us move on knowing that in Christ Jesus we can do all things because He makes us strong (see Phil. 4:13). May God bless you as you continue in faith with joy and fervour, and the strength of the Holy Spirit.

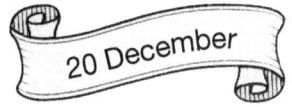

A Beautiful Song

Mary said: "My soul magnifies the Lord, and my spirit has rejoiced in God my Savior."

~ Luke 1:46-47

In Luke 1:46-55 we read the beautiful song of Mary, the mother of Jesus. As I read this song I realise one thing: Mary was obviously the most blessed woman who has ever walked on the face of this earth.

God is looking for thankful servants. That might be one of the main reasons why the Lord chose Mary to be the mother of Jesus as she had a wonderful appreciation for the gift that God had given to her. The gift of being able to carry the Son of God in her womb for nine months. An unbelievable blessing.

If you sit down and count your blessings as Mary did, you will see that God has blessed you immensely. He has given you victory over many battles this past year. He has filled you with good things and He has helped you to see the year through.

This festive season, let us be grateful and thankful for what Jesus Christ has done for us. Truly, my dear friend, if it was not for Christmas where would we be? We would have no hope, no future, and we would have no understanding of the true meaning of gratitude and grace.

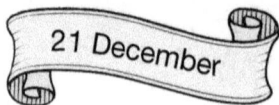

The Christmas Story

"And this will be the sign to you: You will find a Babe wrapped in swaddling cloths, lying in a manger."

~ Luke 2:12

Take time to sit and contemplate what Jesus has done for you and me. He descended from His throne in Heaven and was born in a stable. His first bed was a manger, and the people that came to pay Him homage, apart from the three wise men, were shepherds and farm animals. The King of Glory was born in very humble surroundings.

The Christmas story is an amazing one. A young maiden becomes pregnant, and gives birth to the most special Baby who has ever been born on this earth. A star directs the wise men from a far off country to come and worship Him, and bring Him gifts. These are miracles that can never be explained, only believed. In my walk with God, and especially the 40 years plus I've spent on my farm, I have seen miracle after miracle happen.

As you settle down with your family and enjoy special times together, spare a thought for the Babe Jesus, who was born in Bethlehem more than 2000 years ago. Thank God for His birthday and tell the Christmas story to your children and your grandchildren. Let it be prominent on your lips this Christmas.

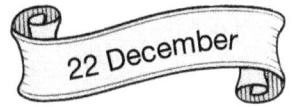

Quality Time with Loved Ones

"Surely I am coming quickly." Amen. Even so, come, Lord Jesus!

~ Revelation 22:20

As Christmas approaches, we realise afresh how desperately we need Jesus Christ, the Saviour of the world.

It is with faith in Jesus Christ that we are confident of entering a New Year with much joy and expectation. Enjoy this Christmas, because time goes by so fast. Spend quality time with your families this season. Christmas has always been synonymous with family time. Put all your problems, misunderstandings and arguments to rest and spend time celebrating the birth of Jesus, our Saviour. It is a time to reflect on the past and a time to look forward to the future.

How do we exercise our faith? By spending time in the Word (see Rom. 10:17). Don't look back, but keep looking forward to that great and amazing day when Jesus Christ will come and take us home to be with Him forever.

St. Augustine said, "Faith is to believe what you have not seen and the reward of that faith is to see what you believed." So by faith you believe for a miracle and as has been stated before: "Without faith it is impossible to please God" (Heb. 11:6).

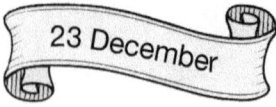

Give Thanks

I will praise You, O Lord, with my whole heart; I will tell of all Your marvelous works.

~ Psalm 9:1

Today's Scripture verse reminds me to give thanks for all the good things in my life. I thank Him for health, for the fact that we live in a beautiful country with a lovely climate and wonderful people from diverse backgrounds. We need to start giving thanks for what we have and stop complaining about what we don't have.

I remember listening to a song by Jim Reeves. It was about a farmer walking and talking to the Lord. He started off by saying to the Lord that he was so upset about the drought, the crops that didn't grow, and the fact that he didn't have money to repair his fences. As a result the cattle didn't have food. Then he suddenly stopped and said, "Lord, please forgive me for complaining."

He carried on saying, "Thank You that this Christmas, Johnny is coming back from the Navy. Thank You that we have a big fat chicken ready for Christmas Day, thank You that we have warm beds to sleep in, and a roof over our heads. Thank You that we can get up in the morning and praise You for a new day." As he started to thank the Lord, his spirits lifted.

A Godly Vision

"Behold, the virgin shall be with child, and bear a Son, and they shall call His name Immanuel," which is translated, "God with us."

~ Matthew 1:23

What a pleasure and a privilege to remember our beloved Lord and Saviour Jesus Christ. There is nothing else that brings me such peace as during this time of the year. People have asked me in the past if 25 December is the actual date of Jesus' birth on earth.

I am not sure and I don't think anybody actually knows the exact date. However, it is a time that all churches and believers collectively remember the birth of Jesus when He became flesh and dwelled on earth. That is what we celebrate on Christmas Eve.

I am a fundamentalist, in other words, I firmly believe in the sovereignty of God's Word from Genesis in the Old Testament right through to the last book in the New Testament. The Word is Jesus Christ in print.

I would encourage you this Christmas to take special time out and spend it with Jesus Christ. Thank Him for the wonderful gifts that He has given to you. He came to give you eternal life if you believe in Him. He has given you gifts that you often take for granted every day. Make a Christmas list of five things you're grateful for today. Thank the Lord with a joyful heart.

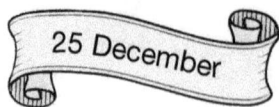

Glory to God

"Glory to God in the highest, and on earth peace, goodwill toward men!"

~ Luke 2:14

My late dad used to tell me and my brother while growing up, "If you get up in the morning and you do not feel like going to work, then change your job." He was a very wise man, because we spend so much of our time working.

Life is about much more than just making money. Of course we have to put bread on the table. But we must also be responsible citizens and contribute to spreading the Gospel to all corners of our beautiful country.

A while back I returned home from speaking events at all the major campuses of the universities in South Africa. The response and turnout were tremendous. One area that really shocked me was when I asked the question: "How many of you are suffering from depression, stress and fear?" Almost 90% of the students raised their hands. We cannot buy happiness. Simply because happiness comes from within.

Let us never be so busy trying to make money, that we forget to enjoy the beautiful relationship with God that is available to each one of us.

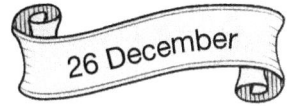

Setting an Example

Imitate me, just as I also imitate Christ.

~ 1 Corinthians 11:1

I remember as a new Christian reading a story about some missionaries who had gone to the South Pacific Islands many years ago to preach the Gospel of Jesus Christ. Back then those islands were full of cannibals. One big sailing ship docked close to the shore of these islands. The captain begged the small missionary group not to leave the ship, but they would not listen.

Needless to say those missionaries were killed, but there was one man that lived. The cannibalistic tribe said that they would let him live on one condition: he must never mention the name of Jesus Christ to them. He reluctantly agreed and lived there until the day he died.

Many years later, more missionaries arrived on the island and saw that the people were very peaceful and God-fearing. The missionaries asked if anyone had already told them about Jesus. They said, "No." They said they were following the example of that one man who had lived among them. He had imitated Christ with his life.

We need to act, live and conduct ourselves in such a way that people will see Jesus in us. Let us be living letters to those who have never met the Man from Galilee.

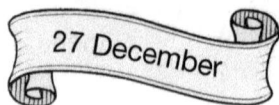

Grow Up

When I was a child, I spoke as a child, I understood as a child, I thought as a child; but when I became a man, I put away childish things.

~ 1 Corinthians 13:11

In 1 Kings 21:1-7 we read the account of King Ahab wanting to purchase a field from his neighbour Naboth. But when he tried to purchase the field, Naboth refused.

Ahab then went home and lay in his bed. He wouldn't eat and turned his face away from everybody until his wife, Jezebel, asked him, "What is wrong with you, and why are you acting like a spoilt child?" He said, "Naboth would not sell his land to me."

There is nothing that disturbs my heart more than when I see a grown man or a woman acting like a child. This is what happened to King Ahab of Israel. He thought that money and power would work in his favour, yet the neighbour was not interested in money.

Sometimes God does not want us to have something. Then we need to be mature enough to understand it, and move on. God's ways are not our ways, but His plan for our lives is perfect.

May God bless you as you move forward. As one door closes, God will open another.

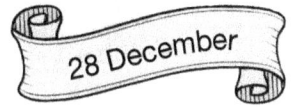

An Honourable Profession

"See, I have given you every herb that yields seed which is on the face of all the earth, and every tree whose fruit yields seed; to you it shall be for food."

~ Genesis 1:29

Farming is definitely an honourable profession. And it's important for me to be known as hard-working and honest. Unfortunately, those qualities are few and far between.

The Old Testament tells of Adam who was a farmer and then moves on to Abraham who was an extremely successful and wealthy farmer. Abraham heard the voice of God and obeyed Him. Then there was Moses and David who were shepherds.

Famers need to pay a fair day's wage for a fair day's work. And farmworkers are obliged to work a full day for a fair day's pay. Without farmers people would starve. We need to treat farmers with more respect, tolerance, love and help them stay on the land and continue producing crops.

Thank God for farmers and pray for them that the Lord will give them strength to fulfil their honourable position as custodians of the land.

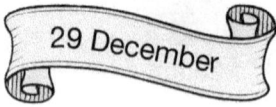

Learn from Your Mistakes

Who is a God like You, pardoning iniquity and passing over the transgression of the remnant of His heritage? He does not retain His anger forever, because He delights in mercy.

~ Micah 7:18

We all make mistakes. Some are costly. Yet if we learn from them, time is not wasted and we have learnt a lesson.

When you have made a mistake, admit it, apologise, ask for forgiveness and move on to rectify the situation. There are many accounts in the Bible of Jesus helping people who had made mistakes. We read of Peter, who denied the Lord three times, yet he repented and Jesus restored him. We also read of King David who made many mistakes.

When we go to God and confess our sins, and truly repent, He forgives, restores and gives us vision and courage to carry on.

Sadly sometimes our mistakes offend and anger other people. But if, when we have apologised and asked for forgiveness, they are not willing to forgive us, there is nothing more to do. Remember, we cannot be responsible for how other people react to situations. So let's learn to forgive and forget because we all make mistakes.

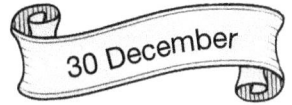

Time to Streamline

In the multitude of words sin is not lacking, but he who restrains his lips is wise.

~ Proverbs 10:19

The Lord is telling us to be careful of what we say. Don't speak before you think and by so doing cause unnecessary wrongdoing. We cannot afford to jump on our high horses. The cost is just too high.

Careless words can cause a lot of harm and pain especially in families. We need to watch our conduct and be gentle and kind to one another.

Actions don't always speak louder than words – your tongue can undo everything you do. Benjamin Franklin once said that the heart of a fool is in his mouth, but the mouth of a wise man is in his heart. So let's guard our hearts. Let our words be few and let each one be encouraging and not offensive.

We should even be thankful for hard times, because such times make us readjust our focus for the better, which leads us to become more effective workers in the Kingdom of God.

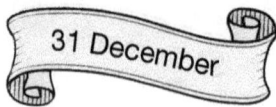

Two Wrongs Don't Make a Right

"You have heard that it was said, 'An eye for an eye and a tooth for a tooth.' But I tell you not to resist an evil person. But whoever slaps you on your right cheek, turn the other to him also."

~ Matthew 5:38-39

There is comfort in knowing that people won't get away with evil deeds forever. Remember none of us is without sin. In fact the Bible is very clear in Romans 3:23 where it says, "For all have sinned and fall short of the glory of God."

You might be thinking, "But what about an eye for an eye and a tooth for a tooth?" Well, we know that two wrongs do not make a right. If we apply that principle, then no one in this world would have any teeth, and everybody would be blind. We really need to exercise patience and allow God to do His work. That is not to say that we must sit back and do nothing. Not at all, but we do need to sow seeds of love, justice and patience. Nothing will be left unpunished, or undone.

When an innocent Saviour died on the cross for sins that you and I committed He said, "Father, forgive them, for they do not know what they do" (Luke 23:34). We need to be tolerant, patient, loving and firm. God is on the throne and we are on the earth. Let us continue to pray for this beloved nation and for nothing less than revival to change the hearts of the people to turn back to God.

www.ingramcontent.com/pod-product-compliance
Lightning Source LLC
Chambersburg PA
CBHW062147080426
42734CB00010B/1587